If Only You Knew

a true story of bulimia, suicide, and finding hope

Heidi Jost

If Only You Knew

Cover design: Jeremiah Jost
Cover photo: Herff Jones Photography Division
Interior design: Jesse and Heidi Jost
Author photo: Amanda Piechnik Quiring

Printed by CreateSpace, An Amazon.com Company

Dedication & Acknowledgements

"Why don't you write? That always used to make you happy," said her mother.

"I've no heart to write, and if I had, nobody cares for my things."

"We do; write something for us, and never mind the rest of the world. Try it, dear; I'm sure it would do you good, and please us very much."

"Don't believe I can," but Jo got out her desk, and began to overhaul her half-finished manuscripts.

Little Women – Louisa May Alcott

This is the story of Beth (Katrina), who lived and died. It is also the story of me (Jo) who lived beyond that death, and has tried in these pages to explain how and why I could go on living.

To Professor Bhaer
and my family, who encouraged
and enabled me to write

I thank God for His mercy that I am still here. "I would have lost heart unless I had believed that I would see the goodness of the Lord in the land of the living." (Ps. 27:13, NKJV)

Jesse, you are my hero, offering encouragement and wisdom, watching kids so I could wrestle through writing. I'm not me without you.

Daddy and Mama, thank you for your heartfelt letters in this book, and for all the resources you provided.

Dale and Lisa, your prayers and affirmation have been such a strength.

Shaina, your wisdom borne out of darkest depression is precious. Thank you for letting me include your thoughts in this book.

Amber, your response to Katrina was so honest and insightful, and I am deeply grateful to include it here.

Gratitude to my friends who endured a dreadfully rough manuscript and offered helpful critiques: Bethany Jepsen, Meagan Hesla, Sarah Bond, Megan Kenyon, Emily Jost, Emily Wierenga, Janny Moore, Abbie Wilson, and Isylla Contos.

Rebecca, you were an angel to edit for me.

Contents

"The third possible path is the simplest. It involves very few pro's and con's and doesn't include years [of struggle] in the future. It is a short path – suicide." The girl has typed out all her fury of frustration at being the loser in this never-ending battle, and now her thoughts are coming forward, icy... detached.

•   •   •

Two cars come down a gravel road, dust billowing out behind them. A dog begins barking in the chill light of dawn. The mother starts awake from a nightmare, and the father rolls out of bed and pulls his robe on. Groggily, they go face the music – but they don't know that it will turn out to be a funeral march. Heavy footsteps and strained voices in the entry hall wake up two young girls in their room nearby.

Mother, shaken by the arrival of these visitors, heads to the girls' bedroom, but stops outside the door to whisper to Father, "I'm going to get them up. I think they need to be there with us."

"Okay," he answers.

The door opens, and the girls stumble out into a foreign world. A bird's-eye view of the living room shows four against three: The family on the long couch and the visitors opposite them. Now who will make the first move?

The police officer speaks up, "I'm sorry to tell you that your daughter died last night..."

Mother turns to the pastor.

What? What? She screams the words inside, but he only hears a hoarse whisper, *"What happened?"*

"It was suicide." Jumbled words fall thick and heavy. "A university security guard found her body... call from local police...researched this carefully and knew exactly what she was doing..."

Mother: A frail body, doubled over in agony. The child of her womb is dead. Sister, who always aches for the hurting, wraps her arms around Mother, her heart breaking now for both of them. Father. He sits rigidly, not believing the nightmare is real until he is told that his daughter's body will soon be embalmed. And then he sobs, and the world falls apart for the other sister.

5

Oh, God, she whispers through her tears. *Katrina, are you dead? Did you really leave me?*

On October 19, 2001, my sister and closest friend, Katrina, committed suicide. She was nineteen, a sophomore studying music and art at Taylor University in Indiana. Her body was found in an isolated corner of the campus. While my family slept, over a thousand miles away my sister's soul passed out of this world.

I have spent these years since Katrina's death trying to understand her struggles, because I want others like her to find hope. I've also battled the same lies that Katrina ended up giving into. In the pages following, you'll meet Katrina and glimpse her struggles, as well as read some things I've longed to tell her. Consider my words to her as messages meant for *you.* If you are fighting some of the lies Katrina gave in to, I hope that what I write to her will help you somehow.

What is your escape from clamoring problems? Is it food, cutting, porn, substance abuse, sex, the idea of suicide? How do you deal with the pain and confusion you feel?

If you are struggling, please tell someone right away. Numbing and avoiding problems just creates more trouble. Find a person you trust, someone who is willing to spend time helping you, listening to you, and seeking God with you. You can't fix your problems alone.

When you can tell you are hurting and wanting to escape your hurt by doing something that might be harmful, stop. Get in touch with your friend/s. If they are nearby, ask them to come over and be with you. If they are farther away, keep talking to them. Talk through your pain, and ask them to pray for you. *Do not be alone.*

Ask your friend to read this book (or at least chapter 14: *Helps*) and then to go through it with you. Some parts might be too much for you to walk through by yourself.

This is what I hope you will come away with at the end of Katrina's and my story: A reassurance that *there is hope for you!* It is found in God. In Him is life abundant. We all need to seek healing in the One who knows us inside and out, and offers us a love, forgiveness, and restoration more deep and full than anyone else can offer. Betsie ten Boom, who suffered terribly in a World War Two concentration camp, said, "There is no pit so deep that He is not deeper still." He promises to "bind up the brokenhearted, to proclaim freedom for the captives and release from darkness for the prisoners." (Isaiah 61:1, NLT) I have experienced His hope and powerful healing in amazing ways since Katrina's death.

In writing our story, I dealt with a lot of anger toward Katrina for abandoning me, regret for all the ways I might have helped her, aching sorrow over the gaping hole she left, yearning to hold her close again, and pain as I probed into the wretchedness she felt. I couldn't keep these feelings out of my writing, so I hope that you will read on with a gracious spirit.

I have found that grief erases some things in its desperate grasping to keep hold of the past. I pieced together real life memories as accurately as I could remember them. Some scenes of our years at home together are composites of actual events, with the intent to show what our life and relationships were really like.

I leaned heavily on Katrina's many journals, grateful that she put in writing so much of her everyday life as well as her inner joys and battles. Anything she wrote that is quoted here is as I found it in her journals or letters.

One

Beginnings
childhood to high school

Dear God, this is your child, Katrina. I'd like to ask You lots of things. Can't we bring just one thing with us when we go to Heaven? What do You and the angels look like? Why can't we really go to Heaven – I mean, why can't our... our whole selves go to Heaven in person? What does Heaven look like? I suppose it has jewels, gold streets, silver, and copper. When am I going to die? I hope I die after my nineties. Amen. Katrina, age six

•   •   •

Katrina – age nine, Heidi – age seven

Knock, knock.

"Time to rise and shi-ine!" Katrina clutched her blanket and kept her eyes shut tight. Sleep stayed for five more minutes.

Then rebuking tones of a loud voice called down the stairwell, "Katrina! We're all waiting at the table for you!" Mama was *not* happy.

Katrina rolled over and looked at Grumpy Care Bear. Boy, life was sure demanding. She sighed and studied Grumpy Bear. He probably hated the chill of the basement bedroom as much as she did, but that couldn't be helped. Out he came, dragged by his blue ear.

Later that morning, she wrote in her journal, "Today I got up late, like usual. I had slept in. Then I got my clothes on, and then I made my bed. I went to my dresser and got my glasses cleaner and its rag. Then I cleaned my glasses."

Speaking of which... Katrina thumbed her square glasses further up the bridge of her nose and unkinked her tense writing hand. Tidy printing was such *work*.

"I folded my pajamas," she continued methodically. "Then I cleaned up a little. Then I went upstairs. I was hungry."

"Katrina," I broke into her focus. She didn't look at me right away. "Ka-tree-na!"

"What?" she snapped. "I'm writing."

9

"I know, but it's snack time! Let's go build a blanket fort quick before we have to do more school. Come on!"

"No – " Katrina wavered. "Oh, okay. I guess I don't *have* to finish journal-writing right now." I dragged out the old painting easel, and threw my small weight into flinging a blanket over it. Swiftly robbed of its cushions, the couch played silent observer to the makeshift easel-cushion-chair fort rising from the playroom chaos. I dove inside. Katrina adjusted the last blanket and crawled in after me.

"Come on, Katrina, before Mama sees us – pull your feet in. Maybe we won't have to go back and do school if we're really quiet." The air was stuffy inside the fort.

Katrina could sound just like Eeyore sometimes. "She'll find us. And you know that we always have to finish our school anyway." For a nine-year-old, she had a low voice. Or maybe it just sounded deeper after my high, excited whispers.

"Never mind. Here. I got this out of the freezer." I stuffed a frozen chunk of Nanaimo bar into Katrina's hand. "Eat it quick." I was already gnawing away at my own Christmas chocolate treat, and making very little progress on the solid square.

The sparkle in Katrina's eyes dimmed quickly. She loved sweets, even more than I did, but Mama would scold if we were caught, and she hated that. It ate at her every time. She sat there, her hand getting cold from the forbidden treat.

Oh, all right. She had to get rid of it somehow eventually, and hiding it in her stomach was better than sticking it back in the freezer.

With aching jaws, we finally crawled out from under the blankets and went to the schoolroom. A glass of water would wash away telltale chocolate. Whew. Safely back at our desks, I grinned at her and we started school again.

Katrina ran her tongue around inside her mouth, picking up the last smears of sweetness as she resumed her journaling. Where was she? "Then I went upstairs. I was hungry."

Oh yes.   She kept writing, "So I hurried to the table. Everybody was already at the table. I was late again. So I sat down. Then we prayed. I reached for the Toasted Oats. It was almost gone. So I took just a little bit. (It was my favorite kind of cereal.) Then we cleaned up. I washed the dishes and David rinsed them. Then I went down the hall and into the bathroom. Then I combed my hair. I had always wanted long hair."

10

She fingered her dark honey-blond braids. They sure were long. She liked that about herself – having long hair. Not very many other girls did. Glasses were something she could do without because they always fogged up in winter, but her hair was definitely a keeper.

Katrina pictured the rest of the day. Probably the usual... help set the table for lunch, sweep the dining room floor afterward. Read afternoon stories with David, Rebecca, and Heidi. Have a snack after the younger girls get up from their nap. Feed chickens with David. No eggs to bring back. Have supper. Read bedtime stories with Mama, pray and go to bed.

•　　•　　•

My parents cherished us. Growing up in the middle of Nowhere, Montana, we had the best sort of childhood. Farmer Daddy would pad down the hall from his office to our schoolroom while we were studying and give bear hugs all round. Sometimes he'd give us a "whiskering" – vigorously rubbing his rough, unshaved cheek against ours – and we girls would shriek and giggle delightedly, "Stop, Daddy, stop!"

I remember going on trips in the grain truck with Daddy when I was little, clutching my Holly Hobbie thermos full of lunch while he boosted me into the high truck cab in the shivering dawn, curling up on the floor by the hot engine. It didn't matter where Daddy and I were going - most of the time I didn't know anyway, but I loved the adventure and the extra spice added from being with my father, who was so often out in the fields when we were little. We'd stop at the grain elevator by the railroad tracks and walk into the office where a bunch of farmers, boots up and talking loudly, would be lounging while their trucks slowly unloaded. Daddy would share hearty hello's and then he'd say, "This is my daughter, Heidi."

With those words, I felt security and the glow of belonging. And I felt it again countless times when, out of the blue, he would tell us how proud he was of us, and Sunday mornings he'd comment on "all my pretty flowers" dressed up for church.

He brought out the fun in us with wrestling matches on the living room rug, where he'd easily throw us all off because he'd won state in high school wrestling, and we didn't have enough strength to pin him down. Bedtime stories were a blast for the older kids, Rachel and David, because Daddy would read each story character's words with loud accents. Breakfast in bed on birthdays was a tradition,

11

which got ramped up one year when we walked into the master bedroom with a tray of food and were greeted by Daddy, face streaked garishly with permanent craft paint and adorned with clothes pins and hair clips.

It seemed to me as a kid that our dad was the warm skin on the parental frame.

Mama was more like the firm backbone. She gave her body to bring us into the world and then to bring us up – through sickness and health, disobedience and compliance. Her five little Germans could be darn obstinate! So could she. Thank goodness, because she and my dad decided to home school us, and it took a lot of willpower to press through twenty years of teaching her children (who often had very grouchy attitudes about learning). Even quiet big brother David could be as stubborn as one of our dogs baiting a prairie porcupine.

I asked Mama once what her family thought of her decision to home school us.

"They didn't approve, but that just made me more determined," she laughed.

She fed us well, at 7:30, noon, and 6 pm precisely, and if we didn't like the occasional zucchini or fish, we had it again at the next meal.

"If you're really hungry, you'll eat it," she said. We got hungry, we ate it.

We got involved in the kitchen early on, learning to make bread from scratch, taking turns making a meal or more a week as we grew older. I love all things culinary, thanks to my mom encouraging us to work alongside her instead of scolding us out of her way. By the time I was six, I took over the kitchen regularly to make cookies, mostly because I loved having baker's privilege to eat the sugary dough.

Mama opened up the world to us not just in kitchen experience, but also through field trips to places like a local honey-making business, a meat-packing plant, prosthesis clinic, bakery, and printing press. She was always looking for ways to enrich our appreciation of life and broaden our horizons, which included speech and essay contests as requirements to challenge our communication skills. She had always been afraid of speaking in public, so I think she subconsciously made up for her deficiency this way.

And when we would pout through school, she sometimes pulled the question that made me tremble, "Do you want to go to public school instead?" The shy side of me shrank and shaped up.

I'm amazed she didn't lose her sanity during those years when she was often the only adult on the farm yard, surrounded by kids twenty-four hours a day while Daddy, Uncle Stan, and Grandpa were out working. There was one day when she'd had it up to here, and took off walking down our driveway. When she turned around, there we were all lined up, small and worried.

On the nights we were sick or woke from a nightmare, we just had to say "Mama" quietly, and in less than a minute she'd come rustling through our doorway. She never complained about losing sleep while her gentle hands soothed our hot foreheads or aching legs. She whispered so many prayers over us. I marvel at her selflessness and patience when I am up with my own kids in the dark now.

Our little world of prairie farm life had one other huge influence.

We had a lot more in common, the seven of us did, than just stubbornness, blue eyes, and blond hair. God gave us each a reason to love and to live. Incredibly, He became our Forgiver-of-sins, answering my parents' prayers that each of us would trust Him with our lives. We grew up in the land of Sunday School and potlucks and quarterly meetings, where God continued to change us to be like Him – a work He did wherever we were... churchy stuff or not. This aspect of our lives affected Katrina greatly. She was only four years old when she asked Mama how to get Jesus into her heart. After that, her behavior toward David and her sisters gentled, and she showed far more compassion and understanding to her family and others.

•　　•　　•

Katrina – age twelve, Heidi – age ten

"All right, Katrina. You can start."

Katrina left her spot on the couch between David and Rebecca and walked to the other side of the living room, turning to face her audience. Friday's impromptu talks were not her idea of how to make a morning good. She didn't like the discomfort of standing up there in front of her mother and siblings and finding that their presence suddenly made public speaking so awkward. Well, she'd get it over with quick enough.

After nudging her glasses up, she clasped her hands behind

13

her back and began to talk methodically, "Boo-hoo, so sad. My windows are broken, and I'm lonely, and empty, and my paint is peeling. I used to be full of life. Children were running in and out and slamming doors, food was on the stove and beds used to be used. There was a garden, too, and marigolds were growing in it. I loved being a house then, but now I guess I'll just have to stand until I collapse. And my foundations are getting wiggly. Boo-hoo, so sad."

"Good job, Katrina!" Mama started the applause. "Does anybody have praise for Katrina's speech?"

In the smattering of clapping that followed, Katrina smiled. That was a pretty good speech, if she did say so herself.

Then Rachel ventured, "Starting out with 'boo-hoo' sure got our attention. That was good. And you helped us see what a lifeless house is like compared to a house that's being lived in."

"Thank you, Rachel," Mama said.

With a sigh of relief, Katrina was mid-stride toward the haven of the couch when Mama went on, "Wait a second, Katrina. We're not finished yet."

Katrina froze.

"How about constructive criticisms?" Mama asked.

"I was wondering why the house was empty now," David offered. "Maybe you could have explained that more. You just kind of jumped into the middle of a story."

"Yes, I didn't quite get that either," Rachel said. "I felt like you could have spent more time talking about why houses are abandoned – such as, the family moved away because they lost their farm or got sick or something. And when you were talking about the house collapsing… that would have been a good chance to explore whether houses last longer when they're being lived in or when they're empty."

What a failure of a speech. Katrina's shoulders slumped. She sat down next to Rebecca. Lucky little Rebecca. She could sit there and wiggle around because *she* wasn't old enough to give impromptu talks and get picked on afterward.

"Katrina, it's okay," Mama said. "This is just part of learning how to be a better public speaker. You did a *really good* job! We're trying to help you do an even better job next time." She studied Katrina's sober face. "Look at me, please."

Katrina raised a dark gaze.

"Does that make sense?"

"Yes," Katrina said, not trying to keep the sullenness out of her tone.

"Okay." Mama didn't think everything was okay, but they had to move on. Her glance fell on Rachel.

"Rachel? Are you ready to give your speech?" Of course she was. How did Rachel always manage to think of everything she wanted to say on her topic, and then put it in a form-perfect speech? Maybe talking came naturally when you got to be sixteen. Maybe oldest children just had the knack for getting things right. Rachel sure did.

"If I were president... that would be a wonderful thing, wouldn't it?" Rachel began with great confidence.

·   ·   ·

Katrina – age fourteen, Heidi – age twelve

"Run, and flop on your belly on the sled – like this!" Katrina hollered as she dove headfirst down the hill.

I watched the snow spray hide her from sight until The Bump, where Katrina bounced up and then spread-eagled on the ground. Why was it that the only time Katrina ever seemed really excited had to be over daring stunts like this? She came so alive at the prospect of risk. I still wasn't sure about this jump. The last time I tried it, I...

"Katrina!" I screeched. "Your sled!" While she stumbled through the snow crust toward her escaping sled, I looked The Bump over again. It wasn't so bad from the top of the hill viewpoint. I looked back toward the house and saw that the yard light was shining through the gathering gloom. Hot soup – probably minestrone - with new bread. Ahhh, hot soup and warm toes.

They're freezing! I suddenly realized, trying to wiggle mine. *Oh well. We have to go in soon anyway.*

I wiped a frosted curl of hair away from my mouth and yelled, "I'm going to try it!"

"You'll like it!" Katrina yelled back. "Here, I'll build it up a little for you first. I kind of smashed it on my way down."

"No, no, don't build it up! I don't want it high." I got on my sled and pushed off. Watching me, Katrina stood by The Bump.

It was too high anyway. After the spine-jarring landing I made, the thought of hot soup was my only comfort.

Katrina shouted, "Wasn't it *fun*?"

15

"No! I landed on my rear again, and it hurts so bad!" I called back to her, rubbing my sore rear as I walked back to where she was standing. "You're crazy, you know, liking daredevil stunts like that."

She grinned. "It's fun! You get better at it the more you try it."

"I tried some of the rides at that theme park in California last year, but they were more scary than fun. Honestly, I don't understand why you get such a kick out of those things."

"And you didn't even try the Hammerhead! Now *that* was a good ride."

"Right. Getting hung upside down and swung back and forth like you're in some vicious fish's mouth is exactly my idea of good entertainment. You're weird, Katrina."

"Some of us know how to enjoy living on the edge," she shrugged. "Come on now. Mama said we had to be home by supper, and it's ten to six."

Talking about tomorrow's sled run, we trudged back over the bumpy frozen field, our sleds hissing along behind us, my shoulder brushing against hers. *What do the stars think of us?* I thought. *We're making so much noise in their quiet world.* Now there was material for a poem.

But before I could start composing one, Katrina broke in, making plans for adding a room to our snow tunnel over by the shop.

"We could dig it out right next to the entrance, don't you think? There's some room there."

"Maybe, but the snow's awfully solid. I get so tired trying to stick a shovel in it."

"We could use plastic bowls from the house and scoop the snow out. Hey, yeah, that would be perfect!" Katrina lit up. "Why didn't I think of that before?"

"I don't know. Good idea, though."

"Well, it would be easier on your weak arms, wouldn't it?"

I sniffed at her tone. "Smart aleck."

"All play and no work makes Jack a very dull boy, you know." Katrina shook her finger reprovingly at me.

"I get my work in the schoolroom. I don't need it outside, too."

"This is *fun* work, though," she said.

We plowed through the bushes by the house, blinking at the strong light coming from the windows. I could almost smell the soup and yeasty bread inside. Katrina stopped to yank her sled out of a tangle of low-hanging branches...

I wish I'd had a video-camera right then to capture her sarcastic voice and bright cheeks, her homely, bulky coat and snow pants, the bulge of hair wound tightly under her hat, our lilting banter. I loved hanging out with her. I guess she loved it, too, because after her death, a close college friend of hers wrote to me, "[Katrina] told me about roller-skating in the empty storage buildings, digging tunnels together in huge snowdrifts, climbing up the bins where you could see for miles in every direction. She mentioned how she loved talking with her sisters. And she said all of this with a greater eloquence and deep sense of love than I can begin to convey. I wish you could hear that from her lips, because you truly were what Katrina considered her most precious gift on this earth."

•   •   •

Katrina – age fifteen, Heidi – age thirteen

We could see her silhouette in the doorway. Rebecca's hollered "sixty-eight" echoed metallically through the big shed. We knew we had thirty-two seconds to stuff ourselves in a corner out of sight and feeling. I was trying to talk Katrina, the master at hiding, into letting me hide with her.

"Please, Katrina? You always find such great places. And I'm a lot quieter than Rebecca."

"Okay, *okay*." I tried to follow along without bumping into things so that Katrina wouldn't change her mind.

"Here. You can crawl inside the tires through that space by the wall."

"I can't fit in there! Look at me." I stared at the long row of grain truck tires and the narrow space between the last tire and the shed wall.

"I don't have time to look at you," Katrina said impatiently. "Hurry up! Leave enough room for me." Somehow we managed. Trying not to grunt, I wriggled on my elbows and belly through the black tire tunnel, and Katrina smashed up close behind me.

After an undercover, "Ready or not," Rebecca came creeping in quietly – very un-Rebecca-like.

"So," Katrina breathed heavily in the rubber-scented air. "Did you know where I was on the last round?" She sounded smug.

"Up on the shed wall beams."

17

"Yep," she said.

"Isn't it scary climbing up that high?"

"No. It's really easy."

"Yeah, I bet," I whispered sarcastically.

"Shhh, I hear Rebecca."

We held our breath and limbs quite still and listened. The feeling of being hunted was delicious – "Hey, Katrina, don't you kind of feel like a Jew hiding from the Nazis?"

"I don't think the Jews felt like this. And the Nazis probably didn't count to one hundred before they went looking for Jews."

True.

"Well, can't you *imagine* it to be like that?" I asked.

"No," she said. "All I can imagine right now is what the kink in my back is going to feel like when I stand up again."

I sighed in the darkness. Eeeuch... rubber smells nasty after a while. I gave up imagining and we both heard some scampering outside our row of tires. Then Rebecca yelled, "Gotcha!"

A boy's voice answered, "Okay – you got me! Let go of my shirt, will you?"

"It's Jerod," Katrina said.

"She got Jerod? How?" Our cousin was a little older – and a whole lot faster – than me.

"I don't know how because I didn't see it happen," Katrina answered, with a "duh" in her tone. How could somebody be so everlastingly logical? Time for a subject change.

"Want to stay here for the next round?" I asked.

"Might as well. There aren't any other better places in the shed I can think of right now." Katrina wiggled around.

"What are you doing?"

"Finding a new place to set my bottom," she replied. "The tire rims start rubbing after a while."

"No kidding – hey, ouch!"

"Ooops, sorry." Her sharp elbow backed away from my face. "I was just trying to get comfortable."

"Well, I have a bruise now! Ow. Oh, I was going to ask you, do you want to play dress up tonight with Rebecca and me – after supper, I mean?"

"I have to finish my science for today." Pause. "All right, after I'm done, I will."

"Yes!"

"Shhhh!" Katrina hissed.

18

"Sorry," I said. "Dressing up's always more fun with you. Can you paint our faces, too?"

"Welllll… all right."

"Katrina, do you like your science book?"

"Boy, you jump subjects fast," she answered.

"Yeah? So?"

"Never mind. I like some parts of science. The book is all right. Why?"

"Oh, because I'll be doing the same book in two years, and I was just wondering."

The game kept going while we kept talking. We made it through four rounds without being found. Hiding with Katrina was always a good idea. Back then, hide-and-go-seek was just a great game.   Only a few years later, it became Katrina's way of life.

Two

Toned In Harmony
high school years

The minds of the two girls being toned in harmony, often chimed very sweetly together. Charlotte Brontë

·   ·   ·

Katrina and I grew very close during these years. Her personality carried the low, steady notes, while my harmony lines were high and lilting. I had a pretty happy-go-lucky personality; Katrina took time to weigh choices and consequences - a perfect balance. We could finish each other's sentences and were almost inseparable. I looked up to Katrina a great deal, taking seriously her comments on the quality of music, writing, or even a person's character. What she thought about life mattered very much to me.

She loved the ridiculous in other people. Everywhere she went, she noticed human foibles, and smiled at them.

After church, Elsa, a true-blue German woman in her "middle ages", entertained Mama for a solid fifteen minutes about her health problems – one eye tears up too much and the other is dry; she's had nose surgery for walking into an automatic sliding door; her knee is swollen... We learned all about the particulars of her surgeries, her recovery periods, and her altered life view (she's extremely cautious around automated doors now).

Katrina's quirky sense of humor also came out in short stories, like this one:

"Jungle bells, jungle bells, jungle all the way," sang Mowgli (who is in "The Jungle Book" story) in a croaky voice as he swung from vine to vine across the Yangtze River which is populated with tarantula spiders, piranhas, can-can dancers, toothless whales, false teeth that the toothless whales have lost, bowties, and gummy worms. Mowgli was on his way to the other side of the river, which is only more jungle. However, Mowgli – whose name means "leetle frog" in jungle-language, and which was given to him when he was found at approximately two years of age in the jungle by a wolf pack of chewing gum – had never seen the other side of the Yangtze, and he was hoping it would be somewhat different from the other side of the mountain. He *has* seen the other side of Mount Rainier, you know, and it looks just the same as the other side of the other side of the other side of the mountain, which has trees and fleas, as well as a few plankton bugs...

He caught hold of a nearby vine and pulled himself up into a pineapple tree faster than you could say, "Anthropomorphization!" or "Supercalifragilisticexpialidocious!" Then Mowgli picked off one pineapple for each year of his life (which came to eleven) and happily masticated them in his mouth. Another way to describe that accomplishment is, "He inhaled them with rapidity and efficiency." After all, that's how many little boys eat, isn't it?

Our hero, finishing up with his kwik snack, leaned back against the branch to rest, which happened to be away visiting Aunt Ruth at the moment. Hence, he fell for a good many feet before a considerate cactus caught him and cradled him for a tender moment. Then his wits returned, and he catapulted out of his cradle with amazing velocity. Forty-seven minutes later, after the pricky-sticky pokers had been removed, he lay down for a well-deserved nap.

During these years, David and Rachel were off attending colleges in Texas and California, which left us three younger girls at home. We had sleepovers in Katrina's room and did many other things together: dressing up, reading, going for walks, studying, talking about what I called "unnecessary trivialities." We were immature and relished it, and Katrina seemed relieved many times to set aside her mental burdens and join our stupidity. On schooldays, Mama often had to scold us back to our desks after she found us goofing off or laughing over a new sketch Katrina had drawn on her desk calendar. I'll admit that my requests for drawings egged her on. I never grew tired of seeing a book character like Pippi Longstocking or Dickens' Uncle Pumblechook leap into existence from the tip of Katrina's pencil.

There were other times, too, when Katrina would scoot her chair closer to me and break into my studies with those tantalizing words, "Hey, Heidi, listen to this – " And then she'd read something from a textbook. It was always interesting. She had a mind for latching onto absurd details. Several of my high school books had her sarcastic remarks penciled in the margins and funny embellishments added to illustrations. Whenever she found a piece of sloppy writing, she soon riddled it with criticism. This reminds me of a particularly good English paper she wrote once.

·   ·   ·

Wryly grinning, Katrina dropped two pages on my desk.

"What's this?" I asked.

"Something I just finished for English. Read it when you have time. I think you'll like it."

Okay, that was way too tempting for weak-willed me. My irritating geometric theorems could wait to be solved; they'd already been waiting a good ten minutes while I ground them through my mental gears. Besides, Katrina didn't often write something that she was happy enough with that she'd grin, Cheshire-cat-like, about it.

Why was that, anyway? I wondered, picking up the papers. From the rave reviews she'd gotten from the rest of the family at the reading of her English papers, surely she knew she was more than halfway decent at writing.

I began to read, "'Dad-burn it,' Marty stormed inwardly. 'Iffen I could jest git this here fire started in the stove, I could start the coffee boilin' fer breakfast.'"

Rebecca, banging her way through a G major scale at the piano down the hall, heard my hearty "ha-ha," and ran to the schoolroom to get in on the party.

"What's so funny?"

"Oh, my goodness, Rebecca, listen to this," I said. Good thing Mama was outside hanging up laundry or else us three slackers would have had to cut short our laugh. "This is a paper Katrina just wrote about the *Love Comes Softly* series. Get this - she titled her essay 'Love Comes When You Don't Want It To.' Isn't that great?" I laughed again.

"Well, read it – *read it*!" Rebecca sat down in impatience.

"Okay, where was I? Oh, here we go...

Her efforts to start the reluctant fire failed one after the other, however, and Marty chafed her hands in exasperation. "Dad-blame!" Trials come thick and fast to those pioneers who choose to live in the wild, wild West.

Unbidden tears filling her pretty blue eyes, Marty Davis crossed to the door of the log cabin, and, her small hand on the latch, turned to look at her sleeping children.

"Ya both be sech cute darlin's," Marty whispered, and smiled a motherly smile at them, envisioning the dozens more to come."

Then Marty stepped outside and crossed a short distance of prairie grass to the big barn nearby. Slipping easily into the barn (besides having pretty blue eyes, Marty was slender), the twenty-year-old called, "Clark? You be in thair?"

Her handsome, big husband with strong arms and broad shoulders and capable hands and thick hair and a tender heart emerged from the half-gloom. Like the dutiful and thoughtful man he was, he had been up since four o' clock milking cows.

"Ya called?"

Marty crossed to him and, looking way up at him, asked, "Clark, could you start th' cookstove fire fer me? It be right tough t' start this here morning, an' you be a right good fire starter."

Clark grinned down at his flurried little slim wife and enthused, "I'd be a-likin' thet. Jest hold on here a minute while I git th' milk pails. Wouldn't want thet ol' barn cat t' git into th' milk afore we do." They shared a hearty laugh.

Soon the two were on their way to the cozy log cabin – Clark covering the distance in long powerful strides with his long legs, and Marty in her attractive self-made dress hurrying to keep up with him.

It is the start of a typical day on the Davis place. Marty makes mistakes, burns the biscuits, spills the coffee – and sobs on Clark's shoulder (or rather, his chest, which is more at her level). Clark pulls her close, whispers words of love against her soft hair, and kisses her at the least excuse.

In addition to these duties, Clark installs new chinking when Marty washes the cabin walls and all the old chinking – sodden – crumbles out; Clark feeds all the animals every day. In contrast to solid, dependable Clark, Marty suffers from roller coaster emotions, "stormings," and (occasionally) faulty logic. But she is certainly not a good-for-nothing. After her first few weeks of marriage to Clark,

Marty figures out how to cook something besides pancakes. She actually becomes quite an accomplished cook, whose potatoes and carrots Clark lauds, and whose coffee – as Clark eloquently states – is "right good."

But the pancakes and coffee grow repetitious (especially the coffee). From cover to cover, Love Comes Softly is merely a chronicle of the day-to-day mundane lives of pioneer families. Cleaning house, planting the garden, chatting with friends, raising young'uns, "neighborly hog killin's," the never-ending romances of the neighborhood's young lovers – eventually it all becomes stale from lack of variation. Little trials (i.e., burnt biscuits, crumbled chinking) test the mettle of the characters, but no single, intense struggle dominates the book and gives it a climax. The entire Love Comes Softly book series features exciting carbon-copy episodes of more boiled coffee and spine tingling, heart throbbing romances.

I had glanced ahead to the clincher paragraph, and now I assumed stentorian tones, and gestured wildly, "Are you yearning for an action-packed, romantic-enchantic, soul-thrilling tale? Wishing for a book you'll read over and over, discovering more every time you read it? Ho hum. Your wish just came true."

"Bravo!" Laughing, I set aside the papers and clapped furiously with Rebecca. "Bravo – so are you going to get this masterpiece published?"

"No," Katrina's face glowed at our approval. "Don't be silly. I just wrote it for English."

"And made our day with it!" I crowed. "Oh, boy, was it good! But what a mean slam on Janette Oke. Naughty on you."

"Yeah, well, one purpose of a parody is to exaggerate the characteristics of something. I don't think that Janette Oke is the greatest writer, but she isn't terrible-horrible, either."

"As if anyone reading this would guess that your opinion of her is that mild."

"This is *parody*, Heidi. Give a little leeway."

"Oh, don't take me so seriously! I'm just funnin' you! I think it's a fantabulous piece, don't you?" I said, turning to Rebecca.

"Yeah. It's so funny, Katrina! I *love* it. But since I haven't read the whole series –"

"Heaven help you if you do," I intoned gravely.

"–I don't find all the bits of humor in it like Heidi does,"

25

Rebecca went on. "It's good, though! Hey, Heidi, read that part again about Marty's cooking. I liked that."

"Nope, can't." Katrina grabbed the pages from my desk. "You have piano to do. And you," she pointed to me, "are supposed to be doing school. As am I."

The Conscience had spoken. Rebecca and I knew that our little vacation was over.

•　　　•　　　•

She grew more conscientious and less playful as she approached her last year of high school and shouldered more schoolwork. Thoughts of entering college and adulthood brought out a tendency to carry the worries of the future. She seemed to find the most comfort in roaming the farm with our dog, Tie, and in cuddling our pet cats by the porch door. Sitting out in the quietness, her spirit calmed. She would lie back and stare at the clouds, happy to be doing nothing. When life threatened to get complicated, she retreated to those familiar, simple things. Katrina was happiest – most secure – when surrounded by what she knew best.

She pushed away the mewing tomcat. "Don't shove, Curly. Tie-dye is already in my jacket and I don't have room for you, too." His amber eyes stared expectantly at her jacket, rumbling with Tie-Dye's purr, while his yellow paws kneaded the grass.

"Okay, maybe I can find room for you." Katrina always took pity on the fork-tailed cat, even though Rebecca and I said he was a pest. She stuffed Curly into another corner of her jacket, and leaned back against the side of the house. She was cold from the frozen ground underneath her, but she didn't mind. The sunset and the two cats more than made up for this inconvenience. What an indulgence to have simple pleasures like these to take her mind off its hamster wheel of things she needed to do once she went back in the house.

She tilted her head back and looked up at the pink-tinged clouds. Stillness entered her soul. Smiling, she remembered the poem Curly had inspired her to write last year.

The fat cat rolls
Right down the stairs.
He does not walk –
He cannot run.
He simply slides

26

Just like a slug
As if his bones
Were made of mud.
He slithers to
His favorite place
A happy grin
Upon his face.

Her smile became a sigh. "Well, kitties, your favorite place needs to go inside now." She gently tugged Tie-dye and Curly out of her jacket and set them on the ground. Quickly, she got up before they could climb back onto her, and walked round to the porch door, where she paused a moment, distracted by the sight of the sun going down over the Rockies. It was breath-taking, she wrote in her journal that night.

The mountains were swathed in a deep but pale pink color, puffed with blue clouds and goldenrod streaks. I wish that following my heart's desires could be my only responsibility. Then I would just sit and think and enjoy the view. How am I going to manage leaving this beauty when I go to college? Would I see such grand-scale beauty there? Or would I have to bang along in my classroom grooves until coming home to see the farm again? I'm probably over-reacting. I will most likely adjust just fine to college and get used to its own kind of beauty.

If Only You Knew
on worry and the future

Oh, Katrina. When you were little, you would sometimes go to Mama and say, "I need a hug," and her warmth surrounding you would fill up your confused, aching heart. I wish I could hug you now, just hold you close away from the cold fears of the future.

At your funeral, someone came to me and said fumblingly, "I don't understand why Katrina wasted all that potential by dying young." The nineteen years you did live were, overall, wonderful and very full. But a lie wormed its way into your heart and ate up your hope for the future, until you gradually stopped believing that God could make the rest of your life just as wonderful. We're creatures trying to control our destiny. Fearful worry bowls us over when we

27

realize that we can't control the next minute, much less the next day. You feared college and what it symbolized – a doorway to adult responsibilities: career, marriage, parenting, managing finances.

I passed you in age and in life experience a long time ago. I think life can be full of wonder and play, even in the midst of those grown-up responsibilities...often *because* of them!

And I know what I'm talking about, because I pushed on and walked into the Unknown that scared you. After you ran to the exit door marked Death, I begged God for strength to step through the door called The Future.

The older I get, the more I feel like I'm earnestly experimenting, living out the life you could have had. I'm living it for you, sister, learning lessons for both of us, facing your fears because many of them have been mine (and some still are).

So here's what it looks like, this many years beyond your death: I have to ask God for His perspective on the moments ahead of me, or else they will begin to seem overwhelming and impossible to face. I've been immobilized countless times by the same worry you described, and every time it takes over, I can't function normally in the *Now*. My thoughts are held captive by "what if this happens?" and "will I be able to handle it?" And then I don't handle this present moment well at all: I don't do something productive *right now* or even make a good decision that could positively affect the future.

"Do you know where constant worry comes from?" Timothy Keller asks. "It's rooted in an arrogance that assumes, *I know the way my life has to go, and God's not getting it right.*"

Satan loves to wield the fear of the future, goading us into a distracted state where we don't trust God and we miss out on the work and pleasures He has for us in the present.

Before I went into labor to bring my first, John-Michael, into the world, I worried sick that I might not be able to bear the pain. I thought about this over and over, but only grew more tense. Finally, on the eighth day of being overdue, I pried my fingers off my anxious desire to control and handed it to God and was just eager to get this child-birthing thing over with! His strange, sweet mercy let me reach that point of exhaustion and surrender. My labor started that night.

For each contraction, I whispered to myself, "Just one more, just one more." I didn't have the mental strength necessary to handle the possibility of twenty more hours of labor. I could only prepare to face one wave of pain at a time. John-Michael arrived much sooner than I'd expected. As he flailed and yelled in the nurse's arms, I cried out my thanks to God for helping us both make it this far.

Life is very much like labor: overwhelming. God knows that our frail bodies and minds can only deal with one moment at a time. That is why He lovingly invites us to "not worry about tomorrow, for tomorrow will bring worries of its own. Today's trouble is enough for today." (Matt. 6:34, NLT)

I'm with you that a future of raising children, paying bills, nurturing a marriage, and trying to maintain a healthy weight is absolutely too much. But God never asks us to shoulder those things all at once or right now. He prepares us, builds our character, and introduces things gradually. I've clung to this promise many times: "He tends his flock like a shepherd: He gathers the lambs in his arms and carries them close to his heart; he gently leads those that have young." (Isa. 40:11)

Years ago, when I told someone that babysitting a few kids scared me away from wanting to have my own children, my friend replied, "Oh, but kids don't usually come two or three at a time, and when they're *yours*, you understand them much better." It's far easier dealing with real life kids, real life finances, a real husband, and a real body than phantom ones!

I've often felt like I couldn't see a day to its end; my struggles (mostly mental) were just so hard. I've let myself become paralyzed by worry, not just about labor pain, but also in imagining my beloved husband Jesse dying and how would I cope? or the unknown challenges we'll face in raising our kids. Will they walk your path, Katrina? I don't even want to go there.

When worry strikes and emotions run rampant, I can still choose to say, "Your mercies are new every morning, God. Your faithfulness is great. Help me trust you." I can look around me for what God has done, and there I find all the wonder I could imagine, and more.

Sunsets like the one you described continue to streak the sky with bold color, then they fade into white-speckled blackness. There's feathery hoarfrost, too, that vanishes under warm breath. Soil magically births green leafy things. Oh, but this tiny flaunting of God's hand on our lives, these awesome beauties, are incomparable to the marvel of a baby and the love that brought him into existence. The first time Baby chuckles, Jesse and I are in raptures. Baby pats my face with his fat hands, round eyes curving up into happy half-moons as he grins at me. Sometimes I lift him way above my head to make him giggle, and while he drops a shower of drool on me, I am captivated by how such a tiny person can bring such joy. When he studies the world, we follow his gaze and are amazed at what we see, too. Baby brings newness to each morning, as his tousled head lifts up from our bed and he flashes four small white teeth at us in greeting. His round sturdy legs hold him up beside the bathtub, where he grunts and points eagerly at the running water. Wordlessly, he says, "Let me at it, Mommy!" This is his attitude about everything he encounters.

And to think that each of our wonder-children came from a sperm and egg that are almost invisible to the human eye! That must be one of nature's greatest mysteries. There are many times that my darkness has been lifted by just thinking about a few of the ways God has not only perfectly equipped me to live each day, but also enabled me to bring new life into the world. His unbelievable care for me comes out in the fine-tuned intricacies of my babies, my own body, and the extravagant beauty surrounding us. He gives me *everything* I need for life. He has proved that he can be trusted.

"You will keep him in perfect peace, whose mind is stayed on you, because he trusts in you." (Isa. 26:3, NKJV)

•　　•　　•

Even now, I don't like thinking about how Katrina distanced herself from us and worked away at her school. She stubbornly refused when we pressed her to come have fun, and brandished her own whip to keep herself moving, accomplishing, crossing off assignments. Yet there were very few sighs of relief when she did finish something. No celebration. Just, "I have more school to do." Katrina was an odd mix of dictator and procrastinator. She refused to run around outside for a couple minutes with Rebecca and me because it took too much time out of her day, yet she would sit at her desk over unfinished papers and long to be with us. I began to really cherish the time I did get to spend with her...

"Eeeauuuh." The frog's eyeball popped out of its socket at Katrina's prodding and rolled across the dissection pad. I leaned in a few inches, morbidly fascinated. "Katrina, can you get that thingy to go back in there?" I pointed.

"Sure. And you're supposed to use the right terms, by the way. 'Thingy' is not a scientific term. We're not studying biology for nothing, you know." Keeping her gloved hands free, she rubbed her itchy nose with her forearm, and then settled down to pick up that elusive eyeball.

"This is so interesting. And that formaldehyde stuff is so nasty." I handed Katrina the tweezers and backed away so that the lamp could shine on our mangled frog. Katrina just looked at me and laughed.

"Interesting enough to try it?"

"Oh no, you're much better at picking it apart. You go ahead. I wouldn't want to rob you of the privilege," I said.

"Ha." Only Katrina could say that word with such a straight face.

"So when we're done with this, do you want to put it back together again for fun?"

"If we have time. We still have to draw in and label the parts on the diagram."

"Yeah, yeah. Hey, are we reading more of that Oscar Wilde play tonight?"

"I don't know. I've got to work on my British Lit correspondence course tonight; I have an assignment due by Thursday."

"Blast Ms. Studebaker and the British Lit," I said cheerily. "Come and read with us. That lady's never happy with what you send anyway – and you always turn in such thorough assignments. I know what I'm talking about. I've seen them." I wiped my forehead dramatically. "I could never do homework like that. I'd procrastinate too much."

Katrina nudged me away. "You're blocking the light again," she said as she pinned down the edges of skin from the belly incision she'd just made. For a minute, she forgot what she was talking about, as she stared at the innards of the frog. She loved intricacy and detail, and here it was in somewhat gruesome glory under her fingers.

"These organs are so tiny and so perfect," she said softly, as if to herself.

"Yeah," I said, moving impatiently and blocking the lamplight, which pulled Katrina out of her thoughts and back onto the track of our conversation.

She said, "I procrastinate too, but I still have to get British Lit done or I won't get college credit for the course. I need this out of the way before I go to college. Besides, even if I didn't have to work on that, I've got a bunch of catching up to do in my journal. I'm three months behind."

31

I knew that dark tone, and felt somehow that my joking had pushed Katrina down the path of introspection again. *What should I try now? The extra-cheerful approach? Anything? Nothing will get her mind off the track it's on now.*

I studied Katrina's profile while she examined the frog's abdominal membranes. That jaw under the smooth cheek, graceful in the lamplight, could take on mulishness with Katrina's attitude. I sighed heavily. There was a place deep inside Katrina that I couldn't be part of, no matter what twist of humor I applied.

"Okay," Katrina said, "now turn on the video again so we can see Mr. Annoying Instructor Guy show us what his frog's nice, fresh, gooey guts look like. Nothing like ours, I'll bet."

The bounce came back into my voice, "You mean *our* guts?" I had to be quick in our grammatically correct family to catch a mistake like that before someone else did.

Katrina rolled her eyes. "Whatever. Just turn the video on. I want to get this done before supper."

• • •

Under all her ironfistedness, Katrina was fighting a secret battle against food. After discovering that Rebecca was allergic to eggs, and that an overgrowth of the fungus Candida albicans caused Mama's low energy levels, the rest of us took tests to discover what foods might be dragging down our health and energy levels. Katrina had twenty-one significant allergens or food sensitivities, including gluten, eggs, cheeses, cow's milk, and wheat.

This seemed to be the starting point of her disordered eating. It went beyond discomfort over an occasionally too-full tummy after Easter dinner, or more frequent guilt about sneaking sweets from the freezer (because we knew we were supposed to ask permission). Her tendencies slowly turned obsessive and unhealthy and then picked up speed into dangerous territory when she went to college.

With the list of allergens playing in her mind, dogging her at every meal and snack, she started to categorize food: ice cream is bad, bread is bad, scrambled eggs are bad. Our whole family embarked on a restricted diet that introduced some weird and some delicious new flavors and textures. Unfortunately, the lines that were drawn excluded much of what our taste buds naturally craved. Gluten, processed sugar, eggs, and all dairy got cut from our daily lives for awhile.

Every time she ate something off-limits, like a donut at Bible study or cookies put out after church services, Katrina felt increasingly guilty. She couldn't easily brush off these failures. She'd eaten *bad* food! Her body was being punished for it, her digestive system overtaxed. Yet what burdened her wasn't so much the knowledge that she was delaying her body's healing process as it was the heavy sense of failure. Every time she failed, she dredged up memories of past failures, set them on the scales of "Good Eating" and found she weighed heavy on bad eating.

She brandished the whip, and punished herself with harsh words. Outwardly, she tightened her control on school. Inwardly, she fought discouragement, as one of her journal entries describes:

I am so tired. Maybe the warmth of my desktop halogen lamp and the sugar in the three snickerdoodle cookies I ate today are causing this weariness. Yeah, go ahead and point a finger at me for being such a glutton. Point ten fingers if you like. I've done the same to myself a hundred times – have repented for my lack of self-control regarding food, and have asked God's forgiveness and strength for future temptations. And a hundred times I've sinned again. Sometimes – quite often – I feel as if striving against this weakness is quite hopeless. Sometimes I hate myself for falling into the same trap day after day after day. Sometimes I wish I were removed from this world and in heaven.

In a moment where desperation for help overrode her desire to hide her failures, she slipped a copy of these thoughts into Mama and Daddy's bedroom. Then Mama responded to Katrina's silent cry.

Alone in the schoolroom, Katrina could hear muffled laughter and talking coming through the wall. Rebecca and I were in our bedroom reading the book Katrina had gotten us hooked on, Oscar Wilde's play, "The Importance of Being Earnest."

She sat there, black, expanding doodles forming under her pen – black as the night outside. Nine o'clock. She sketched a cartoon face, and stared at it. Then she looked over at the British Lit papers spread out by her elbow.

"Blast Ms. Studebaker," she whispered. "Blast British Lit." How could Heidi say it so glibly?

The schoolroom door creaked. Katrina's inward groan creaked a little, too. Mama had just come in – probably to see how

Katrina was getting along with her work – and wouldn't be happy to find out that she was getting along to nowhere. Those big blue eyes of Mama's could pin down a culprit and make him feel proper remorse, but right now, Katrina wished that she could see the more lovable sparkle play in Mama's eyes. She already felt guilty enough as it was.

Mama's gentleness surprised Katrina. "I'd like to talk to you for a little bit. Are you in the middle of school?"

"Umm, uh, no."

"Aren't you finished with British Lit yet?" Mama asked, her tone moving toward disappointment.

"No," Katrina said sullenly.

Mama sighed, pulled up a chair and sat down. "We need to talk about that first then."

Oh, boy. Katrina began to bristle.

Mama said, "I guess I just don't understand how you can start school at the same time in the morning that Heidi and Rebecca do, and yet not be finished by bedtime. I know that your workload is heavier because of this college course, but I've often taken care of your dish duty and some other chores so you could use that extra time to study. What is wrong?"

For a moment, Katrina waffled between two responses. She could get Mama off her back (which already felt knotted and strained from bending over the desk for hours on end) by admitting to procrastinating, apologizing, and then promising to work harder. It'd be a simple, dry reply. Or she could say all the things that were welling up inside her, pressing against her eyes as hot tears. Before she could stop it, everything came out.

"It's because I procrastinate so much. I *know* that," she half-spat out the words, even as she tried to bite back the wobble in her voice. "But I can't stand this pressure. It is so hard on me. I try and try to get things done, but on every assignment I turn in for literature, Ms. Studebaker never even acknowledges the effort I've put into my homework. I have an hour of piano practice in the morning, half-an-hour of relaxing my back with an ice pack on it – but it never really relaxes me, all my other regular courses, plus another hour of practice in the afternoon, and somewhere in there I have to try to fit in some exercise. Often I don't get to go, though, because there is so much left for me to do inside. It is so hard, Mama..." she stopped abruptly, angrily swiping at the tears on her cheeks and glared at the dark doodles on her desktop calendar.

34

Mama reached out a hand to lovingly squeeze Katrina's shoulder. "Yes, it *is* a lot. I know that, too. I want to do anything I can to help you, I really do. That's why I let you off dishes and cleaning. But I also want *you* to do what you can to help yourself. And pushing things back till later isn't going to take off any of the pressures you just listed."

"Well then, how am I supposed to just stop procrastinating? I feel like I have no life outside of schoolwork right now. Should my whole senior year be like this? It's my fault. I have so little self-control."

"How about if you make up a daily schedule of what to do when and how much time to spend on it? Would that help?"

"I can try, but things like that never seem to last very long."

"Don't condemn it before you've tried, Katrina."

"But school isn't the only thing," Katrina took the plunge.

"That's what I came in here to talk about," Mama said. She held out the copy of Katrina's journal entry. "I read this last night and have been thinking about it all day."

"Look at me, Katrina," she said. Katrina forced herself to meet Mama's gaze. Those blue eyes were full of warm love that melted Katrina's embarrassment and defenses.

"Sweetheart, I'm so glad you felt free to share this with me. I know it was probably really hard to. And I want to understand better what prompted you to say these things. Have you been feeling this way about food for a long time?"

Katrina answered, "Well, yes, probably for a year – maybe two."

"Do you know why?"

"I'm not sure," Katrina shrugged. "It just feels like these strong fingers of temptation slide around me and push me toward an extra bite or more of dessert. I know the sugar is bad for me, and that it's wrong to overeat – even if it's healthy food. When I think about how wrong it is, I get so discouraged because I failed again."

"Do you think that this is because your allergy diet is so restrictive – you just want more foods that you can't have?"

"Well, yes, maybe that. But I also overeat the foods I am allowed to eat. I can't seem to strike a balance, even though I know that gluttony is wrong."

"Does it seem like a shameful thing?" Mama asked.

"Yes, it does."

"Please don't ever let that feeling keep you from talking to

35

me about it! I *want* to know what my children are struggling with, so that I can help them."

Old memories flashed before her as she talked. When she was about Katrina's age, she too had lived immoderately around food, but her problem was that she didn't eat. Would it help to tell Katrina this now? She wavered.

"Katrina?"

"Yes?"

"Why don't we pray about this?"

"Okay."

"Heavenly Father, I ask that You would help Katrina in her difficult struggles right now. Help her to see that You are always right there next to her, ready to give her wisdom and self-control when she needs it. Help her to lean on Your strength to build good habits of working till the job is done, and eating till she's satisfied. Lord, I just pray that You'd help me, too, to know how to encourage Katrina as she faces so many challenges. Thank You for all that Katrina *is* accomplishing in her schoolwork, and help us both to focus on that. In Your name, Amen."

She raised her bowed head. "About your struggles with food… after reading your journal entry, I thought of a way that could help you at mealtimes and in between."

"Okay…?" Katrina replied.

"Well, how about if, at meals, you try to serve yourself as much as you think you can eat, and then don't take any extra food? Making a practice of this might keep you from eating past your 'full' limit."

"I'll give it a try, and see what happens, I guess," Katrina said.

"I think it'll help. And for tiredness you often feel, I think you should walk to the creek and back every day for a week and see if that helps your energy level. If it does, then you should do it regularly. All right?"

"All right."

"Good," Mama smiled. "And anytime, Katrina – I mean *anytime* – you can come to me when you feel stuck with your eating habits or procrastinating, and I will do whatever I can to help you."

"Okay." She watched Mama stand up. What strong determination drove that slender person! Then Mama's arms were around her, holding her tight, and Katrina felt the strong love that also lived in Mama's slight person.

"I sure love you, Katrina."

Katrina gave her a squeeze and said, "Love you, too. And thank you."

Three

Brick Walls, Fiery Angels, and Famine
summer after graduation

*I am slowly adjusting to this hectic, harried life. I will freely
tell you that I cried on Tuesday evening and also yesterday
evening....I feel so far from you. I wish I could be home right now,
not having to deal with all this new class stuff.* Katrina, in a letter to
the family

.   .   .

"Please pass the fruit," I said. Katrina sat silently next to me,
picking at the island of cereal in her bowlful of milk. "It's going to
be weird not having you here this summer."

Katrina set down her spoon abruptly and handed me the
cherries.

I knew I'd said the wrong thing. "I'm sorry, Katrina."

I almost reached out and put my arm around her, but didn't,
because, after all, we were the No-Touchy-Touch girls. We made a
point of *not* being as affectionate as Rebecca was. But these were
desperate days; I wouldn't be seeing much of my good friend for a
long time. Katrina was leaving by train to take summer classes at
Taylor University in Indiana. And only scant weeks after getting
home from that, she'd be returning to Taylor to start as a freshman in
fall courses.

"It's okay." Her face said otherwise.

When we said goodbye at the train station, Katrina doled out
the hugs. There was love in them, not duty, but she somehow
disguised the love as duty. Afraid to let the dam burst, maybe?
Maybe.

Mama cried. I tried not to.

Our homebody boarded the train, while I stood there,
wishing I could pull her back and make her stay. She didn't really
want to go.

People shouted to each other over the squeal and bellow of
the train. It was a hot day. Katrina's face appeared in a coach
window high above us. She sat down, sweeping her bangs away from
her sweaty forehead, then waved at us. Oh, she couldn't go! I didn't

want her to. I didn't like the picture of me sitting alone in my usual spot at the dining room table, without Katrina beside me. I liked Katrina next to me. She sat tall and stiff-straight; I sprawled, elbows and knees all unladylike.

Katrina's eyes blurred with tears as she looked at us from her lofty seat. The train took forever to leave.

"I won't exactly be Mother Teresa when I get home," Katrina wryly wrote to us, "but hopefully I'll be a slightly better person because of Summer Honors."

Summer had wound down into harvest time when she came back, lugging suitcases in each hand. She told me later about the other baggage she had brought home with her. They were strangers to me, these weighty burdens called bingeing and purging. Katrina gave me her journal one day, and asked me to read a certain entry, saying that it explained some of what she discovered at summer school.

"Okay," I said. I wondered why she was making this a momentous thing. Then I began to read.

I am at my desk in my dorm room and am so angry at myself. It is infuriating that I cannot control my appetite – that I eat when not hungry, that I eat desserts high in sugar, that I eat and eat and eat. I buy from the vending machines and, heavy with guilt, eat in private, hoping no one sees. I stare at the pie slices, the thick fudge squares, the sweet iced doughnuts, the fruit pastries, the smooth puddings in the dining commons, and I tell myself no. But I take and eat anyway. And my heart sinks with its burden of guilt. When I am satisfied at mealtimes and there is still more on my plate, I say to myself, "Stop, eat no more." But I do anyway, and leave the table with a heavy heart and heavy stomach. I am angry. I have no self-control. I HATE this. What good does prayer do anyway? I need something physical – a brick wall, a fiery angel, a famine – to prevent myself from eating wrong... because I have no strength within. Food fills my thoughts always. I am forever thinking about the next meal and trying to arrange in my mind a nice, *small* meal on my cafeteria tray, hoping that this ideal vision will come about. It seldom does.

You don't know how many times I have asked God to help me regarding this. Several times a day my pleas go up to God, who must be thoroughly sick and tired of this weak-willed glutton by now. I am also sick of this thing. I ate food this evening when I wasn't hungry, and then went downstairs to the bathroom, where with some endeavoring I made myself throw up a little of my stomach's contents. A red-eyed, teary, dribble-mouthed face gazed back at me in the mirror when I finished at the toilet.

How can I control this? It has been escalating over the past four weeks as I've been away from home. Yes, I know that verse: "Watch and pray, lest you fall into temptation. The spirit is willing, but the flesh is weak" (Mark 14:38). I also know that other verse, "I can do all things through Christ who strengthens me" (Phil. 4:13). I must corral myself, especially my wandering gaze and reaching hand. I have to stop this. I'm already miserable; it's the worst life when you can't live with yourself.

Do help me, God. I can't help myself...

Wow. Katrina always took things pretty seriously, but this was off the charts. For once, I didn't have a flippant five seconds of advice to offer.

Where did all of *this* come from? What super-sensitive, self-loathing person wrote these things? Not Katrina, surely. I had never heard Katrina talk about struggling with overeating. She must have messed up her allergy diet now and then while she was at summer school, and wrote this confession of guilt afterward.

"So... It couldn't have been that bad? Was it?" My eyes pleaded for her to say, "No, it wasn't. I guess I took it too seriously."

"Heidi, I tried to express there as honestly as I could what I was struggling with. It *was* that bad. It was horrible."

"Well, now that you're home, you'll be back on the right diet and it won't be such a problem, right?"

She shrugged. "I don't know. It became such a bad habit – eating more than I should – plus stuff I was allergic to. I tried so hard to break those habits this summer, but I kept giving into temptation."

"I want to help you, but I don't know what to do."

"I don't know either."

"Thank you for letting me read that, though. That must have been hard for you, letting me on the inside to see this."

"Yeah. Yeah, it was – it is."

I sensed her humiliation, and started talking about something else. I thought I was being compassionate.

41

If Only You Knew
on disordered eating

My sweet sister. If I could roll back time, I would be a different friend, not helpless and silent, offering hollow sympathy. There is help! And a way out that doesn't require fiery angels or brick walls.

Food is a genuine pleasure, but it can be twisted into a destructive pleasure. You thought food was your enemy, holding you captive. If you just tried harder, you could beat it. You could wrestle control back into your court, maintain weight, and continue your image of having it (mostly) together. After downing that pie, those puddings, donuts, or fudge, you thought that by vomiting, you were freeing yourself from the consequences of overeating, but you were actually becoming enslaved to something much worse.

Eating disorders are a slow form of suicide.

Life spans shorten as bodies begin to devour themselves, seeking enough nutrition for muscle, nerve, brain, and organ function. Teeth and the tissues of the esophagus and mouth are literally eaten into by hydrochloric acid that comes up from the stomach with every vomiting purge. Those who purge with overdoses of laxatives are in danger of heart failure from the drugs. Some disordered eaters try a seemingly less messy, destructive way of losing weight, by taking thyroid medication that revs their metabolism, but this throws off the balance of every cell in their body.

Your period stopped, and you swung from hypothyroid to borderline hyperthyroid. You had some constipation because you had vomited up so much fluid and fiber with your food. Your depression seemed to have some roots in hormonal imbalance from your yo-yo diet of high-calorie binges alternating with several days of no eating. I imagine studying was challenging, too, because your brain wasn't getting enough balanced, regular food.

We are made to crave. This is a good thing! Don't deny it, don't try to stuff it away under a pile of food! Geneen Roth says, "Women turn to food when they are hungry because they *are* hungry for something they can't name: a connection to what is beyond the concerns of daily life... But replacing the hunger for divine connection with Double Stuf Oreos is like giving a glass of sand to a person dying of thirst. It creates more thirst, more panic."

"We were "made for more," adds Lysa TerKeurst.

Is it possible that you weren't finding freedom from food addiction because your motive was to get back control of your life rather than to surrender control to the One who made you for more and better things? His power alone could restore you to full, free living. It seemed more important to you to take charge of your disordered eating so that you wouldn't get fat. You give a glimpse of part of what drove you: "I hate obesity among humans. It's disgusting. All that fat blubbering on a frame not intended to carry so much weight. And almost half the American population is overweight. I don't want to end up there. But I will if I don't quit my eating problem."

We are made for more, true. The thing is, we are made for more than we could ever achieve on our own strength, by our own yanking on bootstraps. We are made for more than just being not-fat. There is a very real spiritual battle being waged over our souls. The enemy who wants to take us down and remove us from effective service for God finds all kinds of ways to twist God's good gifts into counterfeit pleasures. Pretty outside, poisonous inside. Satan masquerades as the angel of light he once was; he is skilled at deceiving us.

If you hear anger in my words, it's not toward you, Katrina. It's anger at the lies that chained and dragged you down and have threatened me, too. It's sorrow at the tears others have cried in front of me over their loved ones who are self-destructing before their eyes. I know the helpless feeling of a sideliner wanting to come alongside but not knowing how, and I also know the helpless feeling of cycling through poor eating choices.

For the better part of a year, I consciously experimented with food. I became more present in my own life, to borrow Geneen Roth's thought, "We're all walking around hungry for an elusive something, and missing the very thing that could fill us – showing up. Being fully present in our own lives." I tuned into moments of craving, seeking to identify the trigger, the cue. I'm craving something sweet. No, on further thought, I want cheese. Yes, that's it. I want chips. I want a donut. Oh beautiful, sugary, sopping-in-trans-fat donut. Why that, and why now?

The reasons varied from the simple: my body needs the protein of the cheese; to the more complex: I'm frustrated by the mess in the house and feel like I failed, so I'm going to go eat a sweet because I at least know how to eat even if I don't know how to attain perfect housewife status. Often, the natural addictiveness of sweet and high carbohydrate foods pulled me, combined with deep-rooted discouragement or anxiety.

Even when I was aware of the deeper causes behind my cravings, I would often still go ahead and eat the food I wanted, following an old habit loop, but this time conscious of its progression: crave distraction from a stressor (the cue), eat (the routine), enjoy temporary pleasures of flavor (the reward) (Duhigg, 2012). Repeat loop. After months of this, the obvious result was still the same – my craving was never completely satisfied. When the sweet flavor melted away and the crunch of chips was gone, my craving was still there.

"God's power is made perfect in weakness," Lysa TerKeurst writes, "This stirs my heart. Weakness is hard, but weakness doesn't have to mean defeat. It is my opportunity to experience God's power firsthand...Compromise built on compromise equals failure. Instead, resisting temptation allowed promise upon promise to be build up in my heart, and that creates empowerment."

Even though our bodies can take on an appetite of their own through imbalanced nutrition, that doesn't mean we just keep going along for the ride. Having the facts makes us responsible to do something with them. We have tools for change. But it takes huge self-control, more than we can generate from within, to shift cravings. Before your heart sinks, hear Paul's words: "I pray also that the eyes of your heart may be enlightened in order that you may know the hope to which he has called you, the riches of his glorious inheritance in his holy people, and *his incomparably great power for us who believe.*" (Eph 1:18-19, my emphasis)

Though God sees our repeated failures, He is not thoroughly sick and tired of us, as you believed. He offers forgiveness constantly. Like the verse above says, He calls us to live in hope! That hope has to come from looking at who God is and what He offers us. It will never come from looking inside ourselves. We are *all* weak-willed gluttons. Even if our addiction is not food, it is something else.

Katrina, I think you experienced a habit loop of eating similar to mine: crave distraction from a stressor (the cue), eat (the routine), enjoy temporary distraction and pleasures of flavor (the reward). We mindlessly engaged in the routine part of the habit, eating to stifle our troubles. Your habit ramped up in intensity when you went to college, where more quantity and variety of food was available for binges. Many days, your habit looked something like this: crave distraction from a stressor like a class paper due the next day (cue), indulge in the cafeteria fudge and donuts (routine), enjoy sweetness in mouth as relief from focusing on paper (reward).

When we recognize the cue (craving) of our eating habit loops, then we can start to replace the next part of the habit – the destructive routine – with something constructive (Duhigg, 2012). I believe God designed it this way, and that He also designed us to transform habits and addictions by His power. Self-control is ultimately grown in and strengthened by Him.

Let's say I'm feeling frustrated with how little I'm getting done today. The house is messy, it's 10 am, I haven't done school with the kids yet, they haven't done their chores, and we are having dinner guests tonight. As I reach for the fridge door, I stop and think, "What is making me want food?"

It's my sense of failure, of having not accomplished what I thought I should when I thought I ought to (the cue). I often justify the eating routine that follows, "I'll do better next time. I deserve this. It's not fair that I have to deny myself this." I make these statements when I am relying on my own strength to muscle myself into a place of satisfaction.

Will my eating leftover apple pie (the routine) resolve my sense of failure? No, it will just make the feeling worse, and cause the distracting, yummy, sugary aftertaste (the reward) to vanish all the faster. I need a different routine when I feel like a failure.

First step in new routine: I need to pray. Lysa TerKeurst said that when she was fighting to change her eating habits, she sometimes wound up in the closet crying in prayer because she wanted certain foods so badly, but deep down she knew she needed God more. If that sounds extreme - crying over food - it is because Satan will use anything, pie included, to try to take our eyes off the only One who can ultimately satisfy us. So I can pray that God will give me power to be fully present in my own life, taking note of what I truly crave deep down:

Him.

In all His great beauty and unending kindness.

In all His understanding, and new mercies that He holds out every morning.

"I need you so much! Thank you for loving me enough to let me fail and see how helpless I am without you. Walk into my weakness, God, and help me overcome the addictions that are too big for me. Forgive me for trying to fix things on my own. I am made for more than this!"

Second step: I need to speak truth (and have others speak truth) to myself, and turn God's promises over and over in my mind. I am not a failure in His eyes. Because of Jesus Christ's sacrifice, God sees me as forgiven. What Jesus did is a pure, clean garment over me, making me presentable to the King. He isn't holding a punishment over my head because I haven't checked everything off my to-do list. "Who then is the one who condemns? No one. Christ Jesus who died -more than that, who was raised to life - is at the right hand of God and is also interceding for us." (Rom. 8:34)

Third step: I need to eat with gratitude. Food is a gift, and God obviously cares about it. Why else would He have put such thought and love into the creation of so many flavors, textures and colors? He takes delight in our enjoyment of chocolate, cream, salmon, beef steaks, curry, fresh-baked bread, soft eggs and hard cheeses, greens, crunchy vegetables, and yes, donuts, too. But He wants us to relish these foods by thanking Him. He knows that our hearts are busy little idol factories, and if we forget to look to the Gift-giver in praise while we are enjoying His gifts, we will quickly turn those gifts into idols.

We will always crave. We were made to. But let's not continue mindlessly and desperately chugging down a glass of sand to quench our thirst. Let's not forget we were made for more than a guilt-laden pleasure.

God Himself calls out to us, "Come... you who are thirsty, come to the waters; and you who have no money, come, buy and eat! Come, buy wine and milk without money and without cost. Why spend money on what is not bread, and your labor on what does not satisfy? Listen, listen to me, and eat what is good, and your soul will delight in the richest of fare. Give ear and come to me; listen, that you may live." (Isa. 55:1-3)

God wants to set us free to fully enjoy Him and His gift of food!

Four

Glitter and Gold
Taylor University - first year

Whether or not you keep up with the tide or get stuck on a sandbar and are left behind, college goes on. I don't fit here, and I don't fit on the farm... I feel disconnected, disjointed, out of it, a wandering gypsy, un-permanent. Katrina, in a letter to the family

• • •

A few weeks after she had come home from the summer honors program, we took Katrina back to Taylor to start her freshman fall semester. On the long drive, I videotaped Katrina and Rebecca goofing off in the back seat, and after Katrina had wiped away the tears of laughter, I asked her on camera, "Where are we going?"

"Crazy!" she quipped.

"No," I snickered. "Long-term, silly!"

"Ohhh, long-term," Katrina mused. Half-joking, she said, "Well, heaven, I think. But in the meantime, I'm attending Taylor University in Indiana."

It is hard for me to watch that video clip now. A voice somewhere in the back of my mind shouts at me, "You should have prayed harder! You should have encouraged her to stay home and not go to university. You should have been more understanding about her struggle with food."

What did we know? Not enough.

At the time, we shoved back the horrid thought of having our threesome broken up soon, and instead enjoyed our last road trip together through Laura Ingalls Wilder country and Mark Twain's boyhood home. Be still, Katrina's beating heart! She loved Twain's sense of humor and writing style and had read many bits from his books to me. Our brother David spent a day with us on his way back to university in Texas. We filled that short time together with volleyball, poolside lounging, and a sunset picnic by a pond. Such memorable, fun things, but they were all tinged with a sense of loss for me.

While Katrina went to orientation, registered for classes, and moved into her dorm room, we hung around town and visited with an elderly friend, Jennie, who'd insisted that we stay at her house near the university.

A few days later, Mama, Rebecca and I headed homeward on a road hedged with corn fields, and I was crying while the late sun glared at me. Katrina had said goodbye in her dorm doorway, but didn't want to break down in tears and so she tried to make it short and tidy.

I hugged her one more time and then she cried. Hard.

We left her like that. She waved down from her third-floor window at us – like some self-made prisoner. Where was our compassion in leaving like that? We just figured it was a natural part of separating, going our own ways and growing up.

While Mama drove, I dried my tears and wrote in a little notebook, "I have learned yet another lesson. Daddy's words came to mind, 'You have to continually give up your family – commit and entrust them to God's care. You never know when one will suddenly be called home.' Though my sorrow at being so far from Katrina will continue this year and gradually abate, it's important to keep things in perspective. No matter how precious she is to me, I cannot cling to Katrina. She is God's gift and blessing in my life, a sign of His grace that I would be presuming upon if I refused to give it up when asked."

•   •   •

"Everyone tells you that school's going to determine the rest of your life!" says Kristen in *Coming of Age on Zoloft*.

College students, observe Archibald Hart and Catherine Weber, "lose the protective covering of childhood and awaken to the responsibilities, worries and wonders of adulthood. In our twenties, we search for meaning, purpose, and our place in the world. Many of us seek out a major in college, exploring our newfound freedom and wings."

But not every young person transitioning into college and adulthood soars. Katrina had a somewhat clearer map to guide her travels into adulthood than many of her peers did, but she still floundered. She observed that,

In the midst of all this extracurricular hustle and bustle, there is a cold hard line stretching from one end of the semester to the other. It is the line of academics: unbending, mandatory, and unavoidable. All college people run into this line sooner or later.

Some scamper from one social event to the next, only to trip over the academic line at high speed and get the wind knocked out of their lungs. Others are skilled tightrope walkers who have learned to balance a touchy schedule of deadlines, assignments, and exams, all while focusing on their goal, which is the end of the rope. Then there are those who hop on and off the line, trying to achieve a satisfying mixture of academics and socializing. I am one of the hoppers. Hopefully I'll get the hopping down to a skill so that I can maximize my time here at college.

When Katrina was only eleven she wrote that our banker "said that the bank he works in might not give us enough money to live on if we don't harvest and get money. The worst thing that might happen from that would be that we might have to *sell the farm*." She was scared of the possibility of leaving the only world she'd ever known. Seven years later, she found herself in a strange place almost seventeen hundred miles away, her education being paid for in part by the farm that was still hanging on.

The money-conscious farmer's daughter knew what it was costing her parents to fund her education, "I look at all the money Mama and Daddy spend on my account and I feel vaguely guilty, knowing that there are so many other things the money could be used for." She chose Taylor because it was a top-notch school to study art and music; quality teaching would hopefully guarantee a quality job down the road. But this came with a top-dollar price tag.

There was extra pressure to score high grades, not just for her potential career, but also to win scholarships based on her yearly grade point average. She pushed herself hard to help out Daddy and Mama, even though they told her repeatedly not to worry about the cost. They were happy to pay. They just wanted her to focus on learning. Still, the cost and the potential career hung over her head. Every day. It was impossible for her to just accept her parents' generosity. She had to earn it. She had to make every effort to help out – and she did. She kept backing out of social events, feeling guilty about not taking time to build friendships, and hunkered down at her desk to study.

There were welcome outlets to the building pressure she felt, as she described in a note,

Dear Lovemypapa, Lovemymama, LovemyHeidi, and

49

LovemyBecca,

I miss you, too! I'm sorry I haven't written to you at all this past week; I have been in a certain condition typical of modern Americans (but I won't say what it is because it's a four-letter word).

There are three things I eagerly anticipate every day. They are: checking my e-mail, checking my voice-mail, and checking my mailbox! Those are places where I can always expect to find a surprise or something nice and luscious.

I intend to write you an e-mail tomorrow – a nice loooooooong one. I love you!

Another time, staid, driven Katrina came all alive after hearing a "spell-binding piano concert. I don't know if I can gather enough of my wits together to write a decent e-mail to you all... The music, played with such power and beauty, took my emotions and my breath away." Then she laughed sheepishly at herself, "I'm only just now recovering."

For much of the fall, her emails were mostly cheerful and positive, as she explored the new world around her and found beauty, humor and unexpected kindnesses amid the stresses. Unfortunately, her work-study job landed her in the cafeteria, where she battled those sticky, sweet, smooth treats most: "I have up-days and down-days, and I eagerly anticipate the day that God brings me out of this Valley of Shadows."

.   .   .

Katrina had requested a roommate who was quiet, tidy, and not a night owl. She was paired up with a sweet, gentle girl named Amber. Pretty quickly, Katrina started to regret what a perfect fit Amber was. Regret? No, it was far more than that.

She seems to be perfect in every way. She is slim, stylish, pretty, and smiles a lot. She has a cute way of talking. She is gracefully feminine and her movements are sure. She's considerate of others and never, ever makes a loud noise. She seems so innocent of anything dirty or vile – she's always clean and behaving appropriately. I can't imagine that she's ever been caught red-handed doing something naughty. In fact, I doubt she is capable of rebellion in any form. Besides all this, Amber possesses enviable

50

things. Her stereo, computer, cosmetics, and *especially* her wardrobe are high quality and expensive.

Now look at me. I am fatter than Amber, though we are the same height. I make noise and bump into things. I am forgetful and have had to retrieve things I forgot to take with me the first time. My conscience is clouded with bad deeds Amber would never dream of doing. But worst of all is my wardrobe. I wear mostly second-hand clothes. My pants are too short, my shirts not right, and I frequently have to wear the same outfits because I just don't have many clothes. (Compare this to Amber's wardrobe, where the hangers in the closet are so closely packed it would be difficult to squeeze in any more.)

So this is me, and that is Amber. The first semester is almost done, but there is one more to go. I'm already stumbling under a heavy load of jealousy, and I don't know how I'm going to handle four more months of life with Amber.

On this particular day, Katrina came back to an empty dorm room and an email from Amber on her computer: "Hey, Katrina Suzanna!!!! I don't know when you're getting this, but I hope you are having a wonderful day. I just wanted to let you know that I was thinking about you, and that you are a great roomie! Love, Amber June."

Katrina's jaw clenched as she closed her email inbox and opened a Word document to write a class paper. But she couldn't focus on writing. Amber's kind words were meant to lift her spirits. Then why did she feel so dragged down by guilt? Why did she hold Amber at arm's length?

She looked around the room for something – anything. She stopped.

Oh, there was Amber's basket of sweets from her mom. Right now nothing would take away the self-loathing she felt. Might as well enjoy the fleeting pleasure of a few cookies.

If Only You Knew
on body image

I sent your journal entry to Amber recently, and this is what she wrote back.

51

How will you handle four more months of life with me, Katrina? That sentence hurt worst of all, I think. It is true that I felt alienated from you during our time together. However, I thought it was completely my fault. I felt insufficient to be your friend and roommate. Your relationship with God seemed amazingly strong. You had a great and supportive family back home. You didn't wear makeup or seem to care about fashion. After growing up competing in various dance competitions and pageants, I felt often guilty and embarrassed at putting so much emphasis on my own looks and superficial things. I felt too uncomfortable with myself to go out without wearing makeup. I admired you for being so sure of yourself and comfortable in your own skin.

You had true talents and could play piano like an angel. I remember watching you play in chapel and thinking how musically gifted you were. I felt inferior to you in many ways, so to hear that your jealousies were my insecurities was very surprising.

I am truly sorry that I didn't know how to convey some of these more honest feelings with you during the time we spent together. I treasured our devotional time together and learned a lot from you. I think that given the chance of time and maturity, we would have had a strong and life-long friendship. I think of you often and who you may have become. You are a beautiful woman, and I call myself lucky to have known you.

Did you catch that, Katrina? *Your jealousies were Amber's insecurities.*

That's something to keep in mind when we envy externals, and wish we had some other woman's fuller chest or wider thigh gap.

Do we really want her entire package deal? Because along with the features we covet, there is a whole life history we know little about. You can't separate the two; they are intertwined. Did you really want Amber's sense of inferiority along with her closet full of style? Her sense of worth defined by pageants along with her slender gracefulness?

God shapes us, inside and out, for what He has called us to do here on earth. He has purposes specific for each of us. Beautiful sister, your five feet and eight inches of person were just right for what He created you to do! You didn't want Amber's beauty because you thought it would make you more effective at fulfilling your role

52

on earth. You wanted it because you thought her beauty and things met the cultural demands for a perfect person. You wanted to be that person.

Comparing and envy drive a gradual wedge between us and others. Our envy can keep us from developing close friendships, because we don't feel complete when we look at the beauty we wish we could have. You made it through those four months with Amber, and came out of it without much of a friendship, because you often neglected or politely ignored Amber.

You want to compare? Let's do some healthy comparing, then.

There are two standards of beauty I've observed: the gold standard and the glitter standard. Which one is better?

Marilyn Monroe, America's sex icon from the 1950s, would rate a ten on the glitter standard of worldly sex appeal. For this reason, she was tailed by men lusting after her, people jostling to photograph her famous body, and cold-shouldered by jealous women. The men took momentary pleasure from seeing Marilyn's curves, but they didn't appreciate her insecurities from a past of rejections, or her yearning to be completely accepted for who she was. In their eyes, she was an object, not a person. The jealous women also missed seeing Marilyn as a whole person and instead viewed her as a threat, competition for their man's attention.

Not an enviable place to score ten on the glitter beauty standard. Let's face it: By this standard, we women have a brief window in our teens and twenties to rate high. But even then, our bodies are always changing through ordinary hormonal cycles, metabolic fluctuation, and possibilities like accidents, illness, abuse, pregnancy, even depression.

I don't know where Marilyn would rate on the gold standard of inner beauty. The watching world never took the chance to find out, because the spotlight on her never probed deeper than her skin. She died young and alone. She hasn't had a lasting impact on my life, except as a cautionary tale against pursuing the top of the glitter standard. I feel sorry for her hopelessness. Trying to have high sex appeal means we have to spend more time on superficial improvements and less time on inner development.

Blink, and the window of sex appeal is gone.

Or is it?

It is if you are just seeking to make your body fit those impossible proportions culture demands from you. Our culture is fickle, its standard of sex appeal is a shifting one. Women used to pad their bellies and backsides because that was considered attractive. In centuries overrun with deadly disease, being fat was desired as a buffer of health against sickness. If women had reserves, they were sometimes more likely to make it through the diseases they were constantly exposed to. Corsets (think: rib-cage-crushing contraption) became popular, creating breathless hourglass figures with the yank of some strings. There wasn't a whole lot of exercise happening for the females toddling about in those bone-crunchers. Yet when women liberated themselves from the corset, they walked right into new enslavement: thin and shapeless. In the early decades of the twentieth century, they began to bind their chests so they would look more boyish, and tried to conceal the womanly curve of their hips.

Full-bodied figures, typified by Marilyn Monroe, were the coveted shape of the 1940s and 50s. A Wate-On dietary supplement ad from that era states, "If you want to be popular, you can't afford to be skinny." An ad for Kelp-A-Mate tablets shows a woman, who could be classed as an anorectic today, looking enviously at another woman who is admiring her full figure in a mirror, and the "anorectic" thinks, "I wonder how she did it... she was skinnier than I am!"

How far we are from that healthy perspective of weight today. Currently touted as the world's thinnest woman, a 39-year-old Russian weighing 55 lb. is disturbed by the fan mail she receives from anorectic-wannabes. She says, "I am not going to teach them how to die. Anorexia has made me lonely, unattractive, and repulsive to people around me." This skeletal woman started down the anorexic path trying to avoid obesity. Now she is walking death and doesn't know how she can get better.

Most of us are found wanting, according to our Western culture, which promotes an unhealthy, almost impossible-to-sustain figure. A study of Fijian girls, for example, shows that eating disorders increased after Western cable television was introduced.

If you want to be popular today, you can't afford to be a normal, healthy weight. That's how we'd have to rewrite the 1950's ad to fit our times.

It isn't worth it, putting your life on the line to achieve fleeting worldly sex appeal. You'll disappear with the glitter you're chasing, and what mark will you have left on the world when you're gone? Do the coveted curvy dimensions 36"-24"-36" fit all that you have been created to be? Oh wait, no, that's not even good enough. Some models now opt to have their hipbones surgically shaved down to meet the thirty inch measurement demanded by the industry.

Kylie Bisutti, former Victoria's Secret Angel model, says that at one point, she weighed about 110 lb. for her 5'10", but she still wasn't landing any jobs. "Do you really want to know [why], Kylie?" [her agent] sounded exasperated. "It's because you are a fat pig right now. You are a cow, and I don't want any of our clients to see you this way!"

"...*How can I be the big model?* My mind was reeling," Kylie says. *"I'm only a size 2.* Convinced I misunderstood, I started thumbing through the other girls' outfits to check the sizes. Sure enough, every garment on the rack was either a size 0 or a size 00."

"In an industry where a size 4 is considered obese, the word fat takes on a twisted new meaning," Kylie writes. "Beauty can be an ugly business."

Sex appeal as designed by God is not a bad thing. But the world's twisted version is. At its very core, it dehumanizes and enslaves women, demanding that they be appealing to all men for as long as possible, and if necessary, to take extreme and unnatural measures to maintain this appeal.

Blow off the glitter, Katrina! It's not worth becoming less than who you are by following the world's pleasures. You couldn't shape-shift into Amber. And if you stop and think about it, would you really want to be a cheap imitation of lovely Amber rather than the unique masterpiece God designed you to be?

Do you feel helpless to change yourself? Apart from spending thousands on surgery or injections, your features and form are mostly out of your control.

But a whole new world of possibilities for change beyond that open up when we are Father God's daughters. We were made in His image, but have fallen so far from His likeness through our sinfulness. He offers us a makeover. We give Him the essence of who we are, and His power can beautify us. We can allow God to mold our character into someone far more attractive than the person we currently are. It is oh-so-not-simple, but is the most fulfilling transformation we can experience.

This is the gold standard. Set a nugget of gold on the table, and although it may not sparkle like the glitter we talked about, it will always be first choice to those who are truly wise and know its value.

If you are pursuing the gold standard of beauty, you are surrounding yourself with people who value you for something lasting. If you are developing kindness, a servant heart, a listening ear, and compassion, these things will draw quality people to you. Among them may be a husband who will cherish you and find you sexy and appealing, even when you are long past the world's window of approval, because he is not looking elsewhere for satisfaction. *You* are his only standard of beauty. Such men exist! My husband is one.

But if you are into looks and dressing the way the world does, chances are that many of the guys you know are into looks and lusting, and would make sub-par husbands.

Corrie ten Boom was a Dutch woman who would rate a ten on the gold standard. For no personal gain, brave Corrie sheltered Jews from Nazis during World War Two and ended up suffering greatly in a concentration camp because of her efforts to protect life. From her pictures, she looks like she would have rated low on the glitter beauty standard. Outliving whatever fleeting sex appeal she had, her selfless example and wisdom have deeply impacted my life. Her warm and insightful love drew people around her everywhere she spoke and ministered. Even at the end of her life, crippled and muted by a series of strokes, Corrie's joy and love still spilled over. One of Corrie's caregivers observed, "Even when she cannot speak, she can reach people we cannot reach...On as many days as her strength would allow, Tante Corrie continued to receive visitors and somehow often picked up needs not expressed by them." Unconcerned with what people thought about her looks, Corrie lived free to focus on ministering to the needs of those around her.

She was given a lifelong servant to meet her daily needs, which enabled her to do a great deal of traveling and speaking. Before that, her servant shrank to bones on the meager concentration camp diet, but unlike so many women today who would have been full of delight and praise and called that an accomplishment, Corrie felt sorry for her servant and wished she could feed her better. When Corrie was finally released, she made good on her wish, and helped her servant regain healthy weight.

You know where I'm going with this, don't you? Corrie's servant was her body. You are given a body to silently, selflessly serve you until you die. This state of the art frame was formed to house the real you: your soul. And you slap God in the face every time you criticize your body, this lifelong servant. Every time you wish your particular servant could be traded for another, you are like clay saying to the master potter, "Stop, you're doing it wrong!.... How clumsy can you be?" (Isa. 45:9, NLT)

God didn't want you to waste your life stumbling around under a heavy load of comparing and self-hatred, Katrina. He wanted you to be grateful for your package deal: the intricately designed servant-body He gave you and the soul that it housed. He saw your body as a place fit for His Holy Spirit to live. He saw your soul as worth redeeming from the muck of self-destruction, so His Son came offering His life, a fresh and lasting chance to be set free.

The more we gaze on God and His beautiful love, the more we will take on His beauty, like Corrie ten Boom did. If we let Him, He will open our eyes to see past the blinding glitter so that we can develop a heart of gold.

Katrina, your friends loved you for you. So many of them wrote as much to us after you died.

I miss her smile. She always made me smile. She was always brightening my day with a smile or words of encouragement. She would occasionally say just one line that would have us rolling on the floor laughing.

We worked on our paintings for what seemed like forever one Saturday. I think she was the only person who could calm me down just by being there.

I remember thinking, "My mother would be so proud if I had perfect ladylike manners like Katrina."

It was like she was constantly absorbing the beauty in everything around her.

Katrina was so soft with people; she truly treated people with such gentleness.

I am a person who is easily stressed about things, but when I would run into Katrina, my heart would slow its pace and I would be comforted by her quiet and gentle spirit.

So many times I thought, "She is so beautiful," not only in appearance but as a person. I wish I had told her I thought so.

Katrina was the type of person who listened twice as much as she spoke. I loved her smile, and the way her eyes would brighten, and she would say in her quiet, musical voice, "Hi! How are you doing today?" And she would stop and talk and listen intently.

She became one of my closest friends and touched my life for eternity. Katrina had one of the most beautiful hearts of anyone I've ever met.

Five

Masked
Taylor University - first year

When I write to you, I feel that I can be myself... I know that you understand and won't take offense. In contrast, with some of my other acquaintances, I automatically put on a façade, allowing only certain aspects of my character to be seen. Sometimes I don't even realize that I'm wearing a mask. Katrina, in a letter to a friend

• • •

Sept 23
Dear family,

On Thursday I did something I have never done before and of which you might not approve. I had a counseling session at Taylor's counseling center. Please know that I didn't rush into this; I thought about it for at least a week before making the appointment. Betsy (who knows about my food problems) suggested it to me. She said that during her freshman year she experienced difficult emotional problems, and seeking help from a counselor was very beneficial. She also told me that her parents had given her a lot of wise, godly advice, but eventually the supply of advice ran dry.

I felt that I had reached the same point: you (Mama and Daddy) had given me so much good advice and told me everything helpful that you can think of...and now you don't know what else to say, because you've said it all.

"You're Katrina? I'm Carol," the woman smiled – far too enthusiastically, Katrina thought.

"Yes." she offered a cold, slender hand.

"Oooh," Carol wrapped Katrina's hand in both of hers for a moment. "Cold hands, warm heart, right?"

Katrina's mouth forced a smile. She had heard that so many times. Even if today weren't in frigid November, her hands would still be cold. The trouble was poor circulation – but why bother explaining that?

"Please, have a seat." They sat.

Carol shuffled papers on her desk, and looked up at Katrina.

"Your form here indicates that you are struggling...would you like to explain in more detail what the problem seems to be, Katrina?"

With characteristic honesty, Katrina shared about stealing Amber's cookies, taking petty change from fellow students, and garbage diving for junk food. She always had a penchant for lists, and here was a juicy one to give the counselor. Might as well make her happy. Carol saw none of the tears that made Katrina's eyes red after trips to the bathroom.

"Well, Katrina, it sounds like the food issue is consuming and controlling your thoughts. Do you think that's a fair observation?"

"Yes."

"You seem to focus a lot on foods you can't eat, and that makes those foods more attractive to you."

Katrina nodded.

They talked for awhile, the counselor putting some things in a new light.

"Okay, I'll try to remember that," Katrina would say after each suggestion.

"Does your roommate know about your problem?" Carol asked then.

"Yes, I told her recently." But Amber wasn't told how bad it really was.

"Would you feel comfortable asking her to be an accountability partner?"

"I think so," Katrina said.

"Good," Carol smiled. "In these kinds of struggles with food, it's so important to keep open communication with people you trust, and let them know how they can help you."

Katrina nodded.

Carol shuffled some papers again.

"Thank you for coming, Katrina. Your honesty encourages me, because I can see that you'll be well able to surround yourself with supportive friends who understand your bulimia. And you do know that anytime you want, you can come talk to a counselor here, too. We don't want you to have to carry these burdens alone."

"Thank you," Katrina said, standing up. "Have a good afternoon."

Katrina walked out of the counseling center and back to her

dorm and began to write. There was no need to force a smile now. When she was finished, she put her face in her hands and cried.

Do Something
By Katrina

Temptation.
The flesh cries out – craves sin.
Stop the crying.
Stop the sin.
Thoughts of sin torment me.
Compelling thoughts –
Stop the thoughts.
Destroy them.
The mind's path is deep-worn
And round.
Round and round –
Always the same thoughts,
Always the same deeds.
Weary, but I cannot stop.
The rut is deep.
I am heavy – hunted – hurting –
Hateful.
Life?
This is not life.
This is misery.
Do something, God.
I cannot function this way.
I cry out –
I crave the sin,
I hate the sin's results.
I am weak, yet
I stumble on.
I cry out.

I cry.

March 19
Dear Heidi,

I got your letter this afternoon and am reverting to a childhood custom by writing back to you on the same day. I remember when it was such an exciting thing to get a letter from a pen pal. I would sit right down with some stationery (often something I had made myself) and write as long a letter as I could. Length was important. If you're gonna send a letter, might as well make it a good one. And if you've got an envelope to fill, why not sacrifice some of your sticker collection (the less cherished ones), or put in a photo of yourself, or maybe an eraser or fancy pencil (hoping that the postman won't notice the extra bulk)?

We obviously like surprises.... We also like being deceptive – doing things right under other people's noses without them realizing what we're up to. When we succeed, we feel a sort of warped pride. Deception has been a major factor in my life in the past few months. I have been a big hypocrite, putting on a show of being a good, godly Christian, while behind the scenes, I sneak around feeding my sins. You wouldn't believe the things I have done in order to satisfy my sinful eating desires. On many occasions I've scoured all the suites in English Hall, looking for available food. If I pass by a trash can that has something appealing and sanitary in it (like whole cookies or muffins in a container), I partake of them. I have lingered after work in the dining commons to binge on desserts, which I later throw up. I've even stolen from other girls.

It's hard to tell you these things, Heidi, because it's very embarrassing. How painful it is to reveal the filth we work so hard to cover up. But I'm tired of this battle. It keeps going on and on and on and on – which is entirely my fault, I know. Like Moses in Exodus 17, my strength is failing and the enemy is winning. I need friends to come alongside me and support me. I know I can share my struggles with you because you understand me, as much as one human can truly understand another. And even more importantly, I can rest assured that you will never stop loving me. Often I don't tell my friends about my problems because I have a deep fear that they'll back away from me. I'm also half afraid of being held accountable for my deeds, because in a shallow sort of way, I enjoy my sin. It takes a special person – one with lots of love and patience – to stick with me as I alternately indulge in and repent from my sin. Up and down, up and down we go. The roller coaster of good days and bad days is turning into quite a long ride.

But I'm glad there are good days. Some of them are very good! Yesterday (Sunday) afternoon I recommitted myself to God, confessing and repenting of my sins. The next hours were filled with a quiet peace and joy from God, and for the first time in a long time, I was truly happy...

Thanks for sticking this out so far. I'm writing this letter in the totally incorrect manner – jabbering on for a page and a half about myself instead of politely thanking you for your letter and inquiring most genteelly after your health. But I know you don't mind. Sisters can do that to each other.

I do thank you for your letter, though. I love hearing from you and Rebecca and Rachel and David and Mama and Daddy. Thanks also for sharing what's going on in your walk with God, and the things you're learning daily from Him.

You're growing up into a wonderful young lady, Heidi! I love you very much and miss being able to talk with you every day. But being separated from you and the rest of the family is teaching me to value you all the more, simply because I can't have you whenever I want you.

Treasure the remaining year and a half that you have at home. Strive to make the most of it, because it will pass by all too quickly. Seek to serve others as much as you can, both at home and in other places. This is an excellent way to keep yourself humble and to become more like Jesus, who was the greatest servant of all.

God bless you, Heidi!
With love, Katrina

If Only You Knew
on accountability

I long to turn back time and be the special person "with lots of love and patience" who rides the roller coaster with you! A lot of people wish that. All I ever heard from your friends was how much they wished they *had* known what you were dealing with because they'd have gladly done whatever they could to help you.

The rest of us are only human, too, and just as prone to stumble. It's a lie of Satan, this thinking that you are all alone in your troubles. If the enemy succeeds in getting you to believe that nobody can understand or relate to your inner ugliness and need, then he has begun to destroy you. He wants nothing more than to isolate you, driving you to despair. When you put up your façade, you shut off the very life-giving help you longed for!

Katrina, your friends could have helped you, but you could have helped them, too. They needed you to be transparent for their sake as much as for yours. There are so many people like you who need to be reassured that they are not the only one facing such-and-such a problem. C.S. Lewis says that friendship begins when one person says to another, "What – you too? I thought I was the only one." A couple of friends who edited this book commented that they not only related to you in many of your struggles, but were deeply impacted by what you shared about those struggles.

Yale student Julia Lurie coined the phrase "culture of silence" to describe the lack of communication among college students about their individual struggles. I think that two deep-rutted habits fed your own culture of silence: criticizing others and comparing yourself with others.

Remember telling about the revelation you had while sitting in a Summer Honors class at Taylor? There you were, in the last row, looking at the back of each classmate's head, trying to think of one good thing you'd noticed about them over the summer. You couldn't think of anything, and it surprised and shamed you, you told me. I felt ashamed, too, hearing it, because we both had the same critical attitude toward others, tending to see the negative aspects of people around us.

A critical spirit, however cloaked in kind notes and genuine how-are-you's on the way to class, is an isolating thing. We hold people at a distance, because we have criticized and found them wanting in some way. You and I were guilty of the shallowness we picked at in others - we magnified the failures of their dress, grammar, music. Superficial things. And we failed to look at their hearts.

You knew so well how to critique; it was a skill all of us siblings honed over the years without even realizing. I think that's why it was terribly painful for you to open up about your struggles, because you feared being scrutinized under the very lens of judgment you'd been using, and - what's worse - found wanting. After three weeks of frustrated eating, you went to your dorm leader, Betsy, and asked if she'd check in on you a few times a day, see how you were doing. "Betsy was, of course, understanding, but I felt very guilty and embarrassed to be admitting to my misdeeds."

Comparing ourselves with others goes hand in glove with criticizing. The Bible calls it foolish: "They are only comparing themselves with each other, using themselves as the standard of measurement. How ignorant!" (2 Cor. 10:12, NLT) When we make ourselves the standard of measurement by which we gauge everyone else's worth, we are on insecure ground, because the standard can shift at any time. Our own moral judgments are shaky. So we grab onto whatever will help us stay at the top of the grading curve by looking for ways that other people are inferior to us: she's fatter, he's less self-controlled, they eat junk food, we only listen to quality classical music, she doesn't do creative things with her kids as much as I do. It's exhausting, this comparing, always trying to be the best.

Here is a bang-on description of us comparer-criticizers in a song called *Fill Your Cup*, "Secure on the outside but melting away... Perfection eludes you, weakness intrudes into your lovely plan to change the world. Someone is better, there's always someone brighter, someone to shine you into a shadow. You can't compete, you're not complete, not when you'll never be the best that there is."

"What you say about yourself means nothing in God's work. It's what God says about you that makes the difference." (2 Cor. 10:18, The Message)

Comparing and criticism are rooted in pride, a state of heart that keeps at bay the grace of God... grace that could be empowering us to live freely, no longer threatened by the good things we see in others' lives. Jesus' harshest words were for the outwardly "perfect," the religious who toed the line and were proud of it. He said they were like nicely painted caskets holding rotting bodies. But to the woman caught having sex with a man who was not her husband, Jesus said, "Neither do I condemn you; go and sin no more." (John 8:11, NKJV) Did he see that she already knew her heart was rotten? "God goes against the willful proud; God gives grace to the willing humble." (Jas 4:6, The Message) I tremble to think which way Jesus would speak to me if He saw me today.

We need to cry out to God to transform our deeply ingrained habits of judging and alienating those who could help us! Let us ask Him to forgive and cleanse our hearts of the desire to be the best that there is.

Changing these old, nasty habits requires awareness, tuning in to the audio file playing in our heads. Charles Duhigg says, "We know that a habit cannot be eradicated—it must, instead, be replaced. And we know that habits are most malleable when the Golden Rule of habit change is applied: If we keep the same cue and the same reward, a new routine can be inserted." Next time I start to tear someone down in my mind, I should hit the pause button. Focus on what I was thinking - what *was* I thinking? Sometimes it shocks me to realize what awful lies I was listening to.

I need to replace the comparing thought (the routine) with a thankful one: "Thank you, God, for her exuberance about life; my serious side needs that. Forgive me for criticizing her size. Thank you for his amazing knowledge of history. Forgive me for assuming I have more self-control than he does. Thank you that I can learn from them. Thank you that they are different from me."

"For a habit to stay changed," says Duhigg, "people must believe change is possible. And most often, that belief only emerges with the help of a group." Katrina, I could blame Taylor University for not sustaining a better community to help you and others like you. But it wasn't the school's fault that you fell through the cracks of their support system. You wanted help, sort of. Your fear of the judgment that your vulnerability might bring held you back from so many people.

You know what makes me cry when I get up in front of a group and share your story? That I can't help you anymore. Can't ride the roller-coaster of struggles and successes. Can't share with you the truths that have been gradually freeing me from so many of the same lies you were enslaved by. That breaks my sister-heart. You stopped believing God's power was great enough to save you, and became more and more convinced that your friends wouldn't want to help you.

Your friend Katie said, "It hurt me a lot to find out how much she was hurting - and it was too late. I always tried to be open with her. I wish she had been open with me and other friends who cared and loved her."

You didn't have to keep feeding your culture of silence, hiding away your struggles from people who would have liked to support you and be supported by you. Now it is left to me to remind myself and encourage others to be brave enough to say those humbling words, "I need your help."

And to thank God that He loves us all equally. Now there's a thought to camp on, "Father, thank You for Your unconditional love that never compares one child with another." When we step out of our unstable place of comparing into the secure love of God, we trade up feeling less-than for now-sufficient.

The song I quoted earlier calls us to, "Come and rest in His mercy, come and soak up His love, come and drink of His goodness, He'll fill your cup with sensational love." Take in the words as many times as you need to. They are truer and more filling than the empty lies you've let into your mind.

Six

Three Possible Paths
Taylor University - first year

[Katrina] thought God was disappointed in her... [if I could,] I would tell her that God loves her more than she thought, and is far more gracious than she imagined. He's like the father of the prodigal son, who embraced his wayward offspring in all his filth, having come running out to welcome him back.
Leon Harshenin, Katrina's university piano instructor

•　　•　　•

Mama answered on the second ring, "Hello?"

Rebecca and I were racketing about behind her in the kitchen, giggling over my dishwashing getup – and making it very hard for her to hear anything on the phone. She snapped her fingers at us, trying to get us to tone down.

Mama shook her head at the look I presented from my latest foray into the dress-up clothes bin: a pair of bellbottoms, a silver shoe and a gold sandal, a gaudy peasant shirt, a red bandana, and strands of my blond hair hanging limply under a brown curled wig. Putting this leg forward, or jutting out that elbow, I kept rearranging myself to find the best pose while Rebecca bossed me about from behind a camera. It looked as if the dishes were going to soak for a while.

Katrina's voice saying, "Hi, Mama," over the phone pulled Mama's attention away from Rebecca and me.

"Katrina! I'm so glad you called…" Then, puzzled, she said, "but your email said you were going to call us tomorrow night because you had homework tonight."

Katrina answered, "I know. I wanted to talk tonight."

"Well, *good*!" Mama sat down by the phone. "If you need us, that's more important than schoolwork, right? Oh, I meant to ask you, how did your *Deutsche* test go this morning?"

"It went all right," Katrina said. "I'll find out my grade next Thursday. Frau Reinlich makes these tests more difficult than the ones we had in our home school German course."

"Oh? How's that?"

"These tests spend more time on the masculine, feminine and

69

neuter forms of words… harder to remember."

"Well, hopefully your German course here at home laid a foundation that makes it easier to add the more complex details," Mama said.

"Mmm-hmm."

"Katrina, you sound like you're thinking about something else. What's on your mind?" Mama heard Katrina blow out a breath slowly. She sucked it back in, and paused for a minute.

"Can you get Daddy on the phone, too, Mama? I want to read you both something I wrote today. And I don't want you to say anything until I'm done reading."

"Is that Katrina?" I said, resuming my noisy dishwashing. "Tell her 'hi' from us!" Impulsively, I jumped at Rebecca, grabbing her in a wet-armed headlock, and began tickling her.

"Tell her," I shouted over Rebecca's screeching and hollering, "that we miss having fun with her around here, don't we, Rebecca?"

"Heidi! Be quiet, please," Mama snapped as she set down the phone and went to the hallway. "Russ! Katrina is on the phone. Heidi, please hang up here after I pick it up in the bedroom."

My exuberance cowed, I nodded meekly and did as told. Rebecca and I exchanged guilty glances. Usually Mama showed more indulgence to our fooling around, even if it did interrupt her phone call. A minute later, we were back at our tickling and yelling. Apparently Daddy also considered us too loud, because we soon heard the office door close.

After laughing herself into breathlessness, Rebecca hoarsely whispered out a truce, and we went back to scrubbing dishes.

As we finished rinsing the sink and wringing out the dishcloth, I said, "Do you think something's wrong, Rebecca? Mama didn't sound very happy – she seemed upset about more than just our being noisy."

The sparkle in Rebecca's eyes clouded over. "Maybe Katrina's having trouble with her eating again."

"Maybe. I wonder what they're talking about."

"I wish she didn't struggle so much."

"I wish she was home." I whispered it softly.

"Yeah." Both of us suddenly sensed that Daddy and Mama were facing a bigger problem than either of us was aware of.

"Should we pray?"

"Yeah."

So we did.

Meanwhile, down the hallway, Mama held her breath as she sat on the edge of her bed and pressed the phone to her ear. In the office, Daddy's jovial papa-tone fell silent.

This is what Katrina had read so far, "I came to a crisis point today. Without sounding overly dramatic, I am grappling with the decision of life and death.

"You know my eating problems of the past year or so. You know how it plagues me and makes me feel guilty. How it consumes my thoughts. How it distracts me from people and cuts me off from God. How awfully discouraging it is." She breathed deeply and plunged on.

"What makes it worse is that I have confessed and repented of my gluttony – my bulimia – to God, and many times I have gone right back to the sin. Often my repentance lasts only half a day. Or an hour or two. Dozens of times this has happened. Every single time I repent, I do so from the bottom of my heart, truly sorry for grieving God with my behavior. But my resolve is weak and soon Satan's snares have entangled me again.

"Bang! We're back to the beginning again." There was no bang in Katrina's voice. It was monotone, like a robot.

"But all is not the same. I am worse off than I was when I first sinned. Satan has now gotten his claws further into me and has me more than ever in his controlling grasp. He has shifted my mindset ever so subtly from God to food and the pleasure of the moment. And the pleasure of the moment wins over the plans of the future. I am angry to see how easily I give in to Satan's beckonings, his whisper that 'It's not so bad – it won't really hurt you. It'll taste so good.'"

"You know that's not true, though, Katrina – you *know* it isn't," Mama broke in. "Oh. I'm sorry. You didn't want us to interrupt."

"Yes, Mama, I know, it's not. But please keep listening." She stopped to find her place, and then kept going, "And he's right – it does taste good. But then after two ice cream bars and a piece of pie and a couple of brownies, I am full and feeling maybe a little sick. A great wave of anger and grief floods me and I go stone-faced to the restroom to bring up what I just devoured.

"The food is mostly out of my system then, but the guilt and despair are not. Usually I *feel* pretty sorry for my sins at this point as I confess to God and promise in His strength to start over. But the

71

feelings change by the next day and I am back in the war again, trying to say no to my fleshly desires but knowing that my resolve is weakening like sand being sucked out to sea by the retreating tidal waves. I usually then sin again.

"I am so selfish. All I think about is food to stuff my face with. I eat properly and healthily in public, but when no one's around, that's when I binge. I steal, too, from dorm rooms and from the library, where I get money for the vending machines.

"Interspersed with the cesspools of gluttonous eating are spaces of wholehearted return to God where I weep anguished tears and long for God to change me. My petty thoughts go round and round about food. The minute I awake in the morning, Satan is right there, filling my head with temptation.

"I feel as if my friends *are* friends in spite of me. That they love me in spite of me. I know I'm not usually genuine in their presence – I have to wear a filter, otherwise the truth about my gross self would leak out and then who would really be my friend?" Katrina hurried on at the sound of Mama preparing to say something.

"I hate, hate, hate this. *Food is my life.* And it shouldn't be. Some days, when I am flailing along in the mud, trying to obey God and be good – on those days I am happier. I feel righteous and my whole outlook on life is improved. But sooner or later, somehow I allow myself to be dragged back down into the pit of the mud and enjoy the fleeting pleasures of the moment. The taste on my tongue. That's all I'm after.

"I have more than once consumed over a thousand calories of chocolate or sweets within ten to fifteen minutes. Isn't that sick? And what's even sicker is that I've done it so often – binged, I mean – that I actually can enjoy it in a warped sort of way. God is becoming more distant with every successive binge. By deliberately sinning again then, *I* am ruining our relationship. I almost don't care anymore.

"So I am angry, discouraged, deeply afraid of my future if it continues as it has in the past. I hate obesity among humans. It's disgusting. All that fat blubbering on a frame not intended to carry so much weight. And almost half the American population is overweight. I don't want to end up there. But I will if I don't quit my eating problem.

"There's more than the eating problem though. How about the rest of college? All the headache of trying to set up a workable schedule. Big exams. *Finances.* I hate taxes and the ways and means of money – I don't understand it. Beyond college there are careers, maybe marriage. Trying to earn a living, maybe raising children. These things are hard enough by themselves. Compounded with my current spiritual and mental condition, life in the future does not look promising.

"So I'm at a crisis point. I see only three possible paths to take.

"The first is to follow God earnestly. This involves truly giving up my sins, completely changing my eating habits, rerouting my thought processes and committing my life to God. After the commitment, the path would not be easy. I know because of personal experience and reading the Bible. God is in the business of making His human creations more like Himself – a process that involves pain. Should I choose to follow Him, I will go through trials that are intended to refine my Christian character. So far the 'eating' trials haven't accomplished this purpose. God promises joy if we follow and obey Him. Joy mixed with sorrow.

"The second possible path is to follow after the world. This would grant instant temporary pleasure. Like eating all the desserts I want and not caring about it. Like behaving and dressing the way popular people do so that I am accepted by them. Living a worldly life like this would be easy because it's right there – all around me, tempting, exciting, promising. It's hard to look past all the glitter and try to envision the rewards God has in store for us if we live for Him.

"The third possible path is the simplest. It involves very few pro's and con's and doesn't include years in the future – years of struggle. It is a short path – suicide."

Mama and Daddy couldn't believe the words coming from their daughter's mouth. Who was this? What had taken over their sweet girl?

Katrina was still talking, "This path would shortcut the longer route to Heaven. By taking my own life, I wouldn't have to face all the hardships, worries, heartaches that are inevitable on the other two paths of life.

"There are only two things holding me back from taking this – the easiest path. The first is the 'end' itself. I don't want it to be messy or unduly painful – or, what's worse – unsuccessful. I would want it to be quick and easy. Less for the people to take care of afterwards.

"The second hesitation factor is friends and family. I don't like to think of how they'd feel after hearing the news. Some might not care, but my family certainly would. I don't want to hurt them."

Mama was trying hard not to cry, but she couldn't help it. The tears spilled out, and she snatched up a tissue while clutching the phone in her other hand. Katrina read on.

"What would they all think? They would probably wonder what on earth could have ailed me so much that I would actually end my life over it. They'd say, 'There's no reason for it. She had a very good, loving, supportive Christian upbringing and a marvelous family. She was even a Christian herself. Went to church regularly, got good grades, was a hard worker. What went wrong?'

"I'll tell you. *I* went wrong. And I can't find the place where I made the wrong turn. Every step takes me further from where I want to go.

"Suicide is probably the ultimate in selfish deeds. I know I'm acting pretty selfish right now, focusing so much on me, me, me.

"But this has to be resolved. I cannot go on living the way I have been. I'm on a seesaw and it's a rough ride.

"God. Yeah, God. There's nothing else to say. The apostle Paul was right when he said, 'What I do, I do not want to do. And what I do not want to do, that I do.' Oh, worm that I am."

If Only You Knew
on life with God

Sometimes when I read these thoughts, Katrina, I just want to hold you and cry. Your pain is mine. A long time ago, Mama wrote about you in her diary, "Little Katrina came and put her head against my knees and said so sadly, 'Mama, I'm really having troubles.'"

If only she and Daddy could have solved your troubles at age nineteen as easily as they did when you were five or six. But we both know that Someone greater than our parents was standing by you at the head of those three paths, seeing your troubles and ready to work on them, but waiting for you to give Him permission.

So you stood at the three-way crossroads, and looked down each path as far as you could see. But your road report was incomplete. You missed the hopeful road signs and faithful travel companion guaranteed for the path of God. You missed potholes in the path of the world. You missed the gray unmapped area at the end of the short suicide path.

When I look at that last and shortest path, a choking

74

helplessness rises inside me. Here was our biggest warning - you talked seriously about suicide. This is what still torments me: if we'd known then what we know now, would you be alive today? People who repeatedly and earnestly consider suicide are very likely to attempt it. If they talk about their suicidal thoughts with others, the danger ramps up even more. And if they have a specific plan, then it's just a matter of when.

Two things held you back: not having a tidy suicide plan, and the thought of our grief. But seven months after this letter, you had found the plan, and despair called louder than our love for you.

Who are we?

I think a big part of you wanted to give up control of the whole mess your life had become (had always been, really), but you weren't crazy about handing over the reins to the God you were picturing. That surrender sounded even more painful and joyless than surrendering to the pleasures of the world.

Michael Reeves writes, "So if God is [holy, ie.] 'set apart' from me, I assume the problem is with him...His holiness looks like a prissy rejection of my happy, healthy loveliness. Dare I burst my own bubble now? I must. For the reality is that I am the cold, selfish, vicious one, full of darkness and dirtiness. [God] is not set apart from us in priggishness, but by the fact that there are no such ugly traits in him as there are in us."

"Those who indulge in sexual sin, or who worship idols, or commit adultery, or are male prostitutes, or practice homosexuality, or are thieves, or greedy people, or drunkards, or are abusive, or cheat people—none of these will inherit the Kingdom of God." (1 Cor. 6:9, 10, NLT)

This is so painfully sobering. We fit in this list as the greedy ones, worshipping idols, giving in to sexual thoughts, abusive, stealing things. We are such lost, lost people. There is nothing in us that can *ever* be good enough to inherit God's kingdom.

Reeves observes that if we see God as only "the Ruler and the problem is that I have broken the rules, the only salvation he can offer is to forgive me and treat me as if I kept the rules...If...some fine cop were to catch me speeding and so breaking the rules, I would be punished; if...he failed to spot me or I managed to shake him off after an exciting car chase, I would be relieved. But in neither case would I love him. And even if, like God, he chose to let me off the hook for my law-breaking, I still would not love him. I might feel grateful,...but that is not at all the same thing as love."

The more we lose sight of God, the more we live by a skewed view of the gospel that involves fruit, yes, but of our own making, rotting on our tree because it did not grow from the Source of Life. That's the frustrating beauty of the Christian life: the blinders are off and we see what is true for all of us, that we need God for every breath and everything else.

The path with God begins with accepting the painful, but ultimately freeing, fact that you can't earn or create your worth. We were made in God's image, and it is to God we must look if we are to find out who we really are and who we are meant to be.

Who is God?

He is the one true God, the God who delights in loving and giving freely. And He made us out of that out-going, ever-giving love He has been sharing with His Son and the Spirit for eternity. He creates because He wants to share His love, not because He needs us in any sense, not because we deserve His love, but because He *is* a Father, so His very nature is one that brings forth life. Creating us was a joy for Him.

Reeves says, "The nature of the triune God makes all the difference in the world to understanding what went wrong when Adam and Eve fell. It means something happened deeper than rule-breaking and misbehavior: we perverted love and rejected him, the one who made us to love and be loved by him... Lovers we remain, but twisted, our love misdirected... Astonishingly, it was this very rejection of God that then drew forth the extreme depths of his love..."

"This is how God showed His love among us: He sent His one and only son into the world that we might live through Him." (1 John 4:9)

He made us His children.

And His great, unstoppable beautiful, fatherly love continues to wash over us, seeking to draw us back to Him with our broken images and be healed. "We have inherent value because he adopted us and brought us into His family," says Kylie Bisutti. "Even when all other roles are stripped away, that's something no one can take from us. God will always be our Father, and we will always be His daughters."

The more we see this Father God, the more we are changed. Faith comes by seeing the beauty and essence of God. When we are stuck in temptation, beginning to think the temporary pleasure is going to be better than anything else He can offer us, looking at the true God restores our faith that He has something better for us. Jonathan Edwards said that "we always love what seems desirable to us. Thus we will only change what we love when something proves itself to be more desirable to us than what we already love. I will, then, always love sin and the world until I truly sense that Christ is better."

Taste and see that the Lord is good! There are moments in my life I've read that and haven't grasped it, and many other moments that I totally get it, because I am gazing at the Source of goodness rather than at myself. We can't see God's beauty when we're busy hating our mistakes and ugly insides and trying to cover them up. We start to believe a different gospel. This is not new. It has happened many times to countless people.

What does God offer us?

In the years after Jesus' resurrection, Paul poured out his life sharing Father God with people all over Asia, and he wrote that he was astonished to hear that the church in Galatia was "so quickly deserting the one who called you to live in the grace of Christ and are turning to a different gospel - which is really no gospel at all." (Gal. 1:6, 7)

Seeing what was at stake, Paul spoke strongly because he loved the Galatians and did not want them to blindly stumble back into spiritual slavery. "Formerly when you did not know God, you were slaves to those who by nature are not gods. But now that you know God - or rather are known by God - how is it that you are turning back to those weak and miserable principles? Do you wish to be enslaved all over again?" (Gal. 4:8,9)

"Did you receive the spirit by observing the law or by believing what you heard? Are you so foolish? After beginning with the Spirit, are you now trying to attain your goal by human effort?" (Gal. 3:2)

That sounds like us right there, Katrina. We knew all about the law that God set in place to show us how impossible it is for us to be perfect. And we knew that He sent Jesus to satisfy all the demands of the law, because *He* was perfect. But we lost sight of that, and in confused pride, focused on "weak and miserable principles", striving to be good enough for the salvation God offered us. God sees that we fail, but that does not make us failures to Him. He sees Christ Jesus' perfection when He looks at us, because we have been forgiven. Christ takes our messed-up lives and gives us, in exchange, the perfect life He lived that we could never achieve.

How good, really, was the life you had? You threw back calories in secret, deep down hungry for something to give you an unshakable sense of worth. You smiled on the walks to class, and wept alone in the dark. I ache for you. What a terrible place of lostness! I know. I know what it is like in my own way, and that's why I hurt all the more at the thought of you being in it, and never getting out.

Oh, sweet sister, "What has happened to all your joy?" (Gal. 4:15) You won't get it back on the glittering path or the short path of suicide. It is only on the path with God.

"God created man for nothing else but happiness," Jonathan Edwards told his congregation. "He created him only that he might communicate happiness to him. "Christ's yoke is easy, His burden light. Much, much lighter than the slave yoke created by our own inward-curving, self-loving destruction.

Dearest Katrina,

I want you to know how much I truly love you. Yes, I have loved you with an everlasting love; with loving-kindness I have drawn you. I have searched you and known you. I know your sitting down and your rising up. I understand your thoughts afar off. I comprehend your path and your lying down; I am acquainted with all your ways. I have hedged you behind and before; I have laid My hand on you. I know – such knowledge is too wonderful for you. It is so high you cannot attain it.

But where can you go from My Spirit, or where can you flee from My presence? If you ascend into heaven, I am there. If you make your bed in the depths, I am there as well. If you take the wings of the morning, or dwell in the uttermost parts of the sea, even there My hand shall lead you, and My right hand shall hold you. The darkness shall not hide you; the darkness and the light are both alike to Me.

Katrina, I created every part of you; I tenderly covered you in your mother's womb. You were not hidden from Me while I skillfully knit your skeleton. I saw you even before you were formed. You are truly precious in My sight. How often I think of you! If you could count the times, they would number more than the sands of the sea. The thoughts I have of you are plans of peace and not of evil – to give you a future with hope!

Fear not, I am with you. Don't be dismayed: I am your God. I will strengthen you; yes, I will help you. I hold you in My hand. All the days I have fashioned for you are written in My book. I set the number of days you have on this earth before you even existed, and nothing can shorten them. You are Mine, little Katrina, and no one can snatch you from My hands.

Oh, how I love you! Abide in My love. I will quiet you with My love, and will rejoice over you with singing.

Precious Katrina, do not despise My chastening, for I chasten those I love. I do this for your profit, that you may partake of My holiness. Behold, eye has not seen, nor ear heard, nor has it even entered into the heart of man, the things that I have prepared for those who love Me.

You love Me because I first loved you. You know, there is no greater love than to lay down one's life for his friend. This is even how you know love, because I laid down My life for you.

O that you could comprehend the width and length and depth and height of My love, which surpasses knowledge. For what shall separate you from My love? Shall tribulation, or distress, or persecution, or famine, or peril, or sword? There is nothing, neither death nor life, nor angels nor principalities nor powers, nor things present nor things to come, nor height nor depth, nor any other created thing that shall ever be able to separate you from My love.

Not even your sins can separate you from My love. Dear one, I wish you could see the depth of My grace! Reason with me, Katrina. Though your sins are as scarlet, I can make you so that you are as white as snow. Forget the former things; do not dwell on the past. I, even I, am He who blots out your transgressions, for My own sake, and remembers your sins no more!

Think about these things, My dear daughter: If I am for you, who can be against you? Who can bring a charge against you? I am the One who justifies you! Who is the one condemning you? I died in your stead, rose from the dead, and I am at the right hand of My

Father, pleading for you! Who does that leave, Katrina? Who is making you feel guilty?

Do you have any idea how much I paid so that you could walk away from your sins and be free from them? Why do you ignore My finished work? I said, "It is finished." There is nothing more you can do to atone for your sin. If you will agree with Me and admit that what you did was wrong, I promise you I will forgive your sins and cleanse you from all unrighteousness. Katrina, listen to Me: Your sins are forgiven you for My name's sake! Your sins are forgiven you, so go and sin no more! Even if your heart condemns you, I am greater than your heart, and know all things.

If I set you free, you will be free indeed. It is for freedom that I have set you free. Stand firm then! Don't let yourself be burdened again by a yoke of slavery. My mercies are new every morning. Accept what I have done. Nothing you have done can justify you in My sight. I became sin for you. I give you My righteousness. When My Father looks at you, He doesn't see your sins. They were all wiped away at the cross for those who put their faith in Me. You stand clean before Me, Katrina. Because of the cross, you are blameless. Believe Me when I tell you that your sins are forgiven you! Go and sin no more. Without Me, you can do nothing. But through Me, you can do whatever I ask of you!

I love you dearly, Katrina.

Your God and Savior,
Jesus Christ

References used: Jer. 31:3; Ps. 139; Isa. 43:4; Jer. 29:11; Isa. 41:10; John 10:28, 15:9; Zeph. 3:17; Heb. 4:5-6, 10; 1 Cor. 2:9; 1 John 4:19; John 15:13; 1 John 3:16; Eph. 3:18-19; Rom. 8:35, 38-39; Isa. 1:18, 43:18, 25; Rom. 8:31-34; John 19:13; 1 John 1:9, 2:12; John 8:11; 1 John 3:20; John 8:36; Gal. 5:1; Rom. 3:20; 2 Cor. 5:21; John 15:1; Phil. 4:13.

Seven

Mountains and Giants
Final summer

> *I challenge the students to identify the giants that are waiting
> for them at home and to formulate a plan to conquer them. Please
> ask Katrina about the giants that she's identified in her life.*
> Gordy Grover, director of youth missions trip to Philippines

•　　　•　　　•

Daddy and Mama didn't tell Rebecca and me what Katrina
had phoned about; they wanted to shelter us from her tormented
despair. Instead, they told Rachel, who immediately wrote Katrina a
long, big-sister letter, encouraging her to remember that "you are
declared His child... all the work has been done for you on the cross."

Just days after her call for help, Mama packed up and flew
out to see Katrina. I only knew that she needed to spend some time
with her, and that Katrina was struggling with her eating. Between
classes, they spent a lot of time together. Katrina soaked up every
minute of those days.

They didn't talk about the three paths letter until one
afternoon when they were sitting on the dock by Taylor Lake.

Mama was crying before she could even get the question out.
She turned red-rimmed eyes toward Katrina and put a trembling hand
on her arm. Katrina saw love and fear in her look.

"When you talked about suicide as an option, did you really
mean it? Would you seriously do that?"

"No, Mama," she answered quickly. "No. No, I think I just
felt really overwhelmed when I wrote out those options. I'm much
better."

She hugged Mama again, and tried to reassure her with a
smile. "I'm fine. Really, truly."

•　　　•　　　•

"Hello, Katrina," Pastor Thom said, shaking her hand.
"Please have a seat."

Katrina pulled out a chair next to Mama and sat down. While

Thom and Mama made small talk for a few minutes, she studied this new person with gentle, careworn face who was going to counsel her. She doubted this was going to transform her any more than all the past help and advice. But she had just given Mama the scare of her life with that three paths letter, and the least she could do was make an effort to go along with this.

Thom spoke good, true words. He shared from his own disordered eating past. He pointed Katrina back to God. But deep at the core of her being, I believe she did not really see the real God. She saw a policeman out to catch her in law-breaking acts. Or, in softened moments, she saw Him as a kind, but distant Creator who wanted her to live up to His expectations. If she did, some perks were included.

Thankfully, Katrina had a friend to go to the other counseling sessions with her before the semester ended. Throughout the spring, Stephanie, a pastor's daughter with an ever-ready smile, had reached in past Katrina's reserved front and won her trust. One evening after returning to Stephanie's room from a concert, Katrina relaxed from the pressures of homework enough to stay and visit for awhile. "I don't know how she does it, but she makes me feel so loved as she gently draws me out and asks deep questions...When I told her about my eating problems, expressing my discouragement with them, she said, 'Despite all that, Katrina, you're so beautiful. I love you.'" Katrina broke down crying, Stephanie's arms around her.

Far away in Montana, Daddy and Mama tried to stay close through phone calls and emails with Katrina. Daddy spoke warm affection for his hurting girl, and prayed with her. Mama sent books and suggestions. Many nights would find her poring over the pages of the Bible by lamplight, desperately seeking wisdom for herself and her daughter.

Pastor Thom also came alongside Katrina, encouraging her to memorize verses about God's help and overcoming temptations so that she could say them aloud when she was tempted to binge or steal food. He strongly urged her to call him or friends or family to get some accountability and distraction from the temptation at hand. And he emphasized the power of prayer: speaking to God could help to focus her on God's desire and ability to gain victory, and take her mind off her past failures. During counseling sessions, Katrina, Stephanie, and Pastor Thomas went over each week's successes and mess-ups, seeking to learn from them and make steps forward next time.

82

Yet sometimes Pastor Thomas's advice seemed so simplistic, so out of touch with the irresistible pull of bingeing on and vomiting up food. Katrina vented her frustration in writing.

Stalking from the house, the girl grabbed an axe from the barn and headed straight out into the woods. Her steps grew faster and more agitated as she went. Then, at the sight of a nearby fallen tree, she gripped the axe, swung it high, and with fierce bitter anger, slammed it down into the fallen tree trunk. Again and again the axe flashed downward, savagely gouging the wood, and sending wood chips flying. Thud! Thud! Thud!

Sweat began to trickle down her sides. Her jaw clenched, she kept swinging the axe. Then, quite suddenly, the girl's passionate power vanished. After one last thud, she left the axe-head buried in the slashed trunk and collapsed weakly against the log. She slid to the ground, weeping. The rage was spent. Only a dull, empty feeling remained in the girl's heart. Dead dullness.

It was a long time before she felt ready to get up again.

Other days, Katrina got a lot of hope from the simple choice to ask God for help and build accountability.

"My heart ached for Katrina as she courageously became vulnerable to our small group [that spring]," said her group leader, Heidi. "Her struggle with bulimia is not an uncommon one to girls our age, but I know that she felt alone in her addiction. She shared with us what she learned at each session. We rejoiced with Katrina as she made progress - tiny steps, but steps in the right direction nonetheless."

Katrina described one of the many tiny steps, "As the familiar flood of discouragement swept over me, and began to embitter me, I strove to stay afloat by filling my mind with thoughts of God's mercy and with the knowledge that I could start all over tomorrow. It worked!"

She sounded surprised.

•   •   •

Katrina's spring semester finally ended, and she came home for a little while. Then she and I boarded the bus for Manitou Springs, Colorado, where we attended Summit, a two week summer training camp on Christian worldview. Together with 180 other young people, we ate, slept, and took our classes in a big turn-of-the-century hotel. For several hours every morning, different speakers gave us truths on moral issues and the big picture of life so that we would be prepared with accurate answers for others and ourselves. Katrina penned a handful of comments in the margins of her big class notebook, including something one of our teachers said, "I am by nature a pessimist, but I am by theology an optimist."

The material presented at Summit was great, but after being apart for months, I probably got more out of my time with Katrina than I did from classes. We hiked up and down Manitou's hilly streets, and poked our noses in narrow shops crammed with incense and crystals. We were even banned from a Western saddle store after hesitantly witnessing to the owners.

I remember best the afternoon we climbed up into the old Summit hotel attic and watched a fantastic thunderstorm from a window. The curtains flapped in the breeze, and we rocked to and fro in our chairs, watching the yellow-gray sky. That pounding rumble of thunder and the flashes of lightning. The colors and sounds were so intense. And then we read Psalm 119 together, "How can a young man keep his way pure? By living according to your word." Drops of rain beat against the roof, and the swirling breeze ruffling the pages of our Bibles.

There's another memory I have to share, because it was a turning point in my understanding of Katrina's struggle with food.

•   •   •

How had it come to this? I looked up at the Colorado sky, trying to clear my eyes of tears long enough to return to earth and speak straight to the straightforward girl sitting across from me. Katrina didn't like tears much; they made her feel awkward, and if they were for her, she felt guilty. I knew that. Then why couldn't I stop gulping down the sobs? How could a cherry tart ruin such a perfect June day? A *cherry tart*!

"Katrina, I don't know how to say this…" I angrily swiped away the tears. Was it anger at the tears or at Katrina or at myself?

"Remember how when we left on the bus to come down here, Mama told you that I was supposed to hold you accountable for your eating habits, and you were supposed to let me know when you were struggling? I – I wasn't thinking earlier today at lunch. Well, I didn't think anything of eating that tart for dessert, but then I – you took one, too, didn't you?"

I went on awkwardly at Katrina's nod. "Well, I saw that, and I felt horrible because I thought maybe my action had tempted you to do that. I went upstairs and read Romans 14. I wanted to read some of it to you, because it explains why I'm talking to you now and apologizing for what I did."

"It's all right, Heidi," Katrina said in a distant voice. "Don't worry – "

"No, no, please, I need to say this. Here." Sliding forward on the rusty lawn chair, I leaned my elbows on the table and riffled through the Bible. I heard the crowd of Summit students on the hotel front porch. Chairs scraped, the swing thumped against the hotel wall, feet tramped back and forth. Though they were just on the other side of a high fence, only twenty feet away, I felt further away from that crowd of teenagers now than I had during my whole two weeks with them. They could laugh with light hearts, I thought, because I bet *they* didn't have a sister who would eat and vomit and eat and vomit – and was becoming more of a stranger every day.

I sighed and began to read, "'If your brother is grieved because of your food, you are no longer walking in love. Do not destroy with your food the one for whom Christ died.' Umm, and then there was this part near the end, 'Do not destroy the work of God for the sake of food. All things indeed are pure, but it is evil for the man who eats with offense. It is good neither to eat meat nor drink wine nor do anything by which your brother stumbles or is offended or is made weak.'"

I looked up. Katrina was staring blankly across the courtyard.

"I know Paul's talking more about the meat sacrificed to idols, the offending thing in his day, but it seemed like this applied for you and me where we are in our lives right now.

"Katrina, I'm *so* sorry. In the first place, I haven't been faithful about holding you accountable and encouraging you, and now I see that I haven't been very good at making it easier for you to stay away from the foods you're allergic to."

Even as I said it, I frowned a little, struggling to understand why Katrina always found a giant battle in avoiding the offending sugar, wheat, and dairy when I found only little skirmishes. *Oh, I wish she wouldn't take this so seriously! It'd be much easier for her.*

"It's all right, Heidi. Don't feel bad. I don't blame you at all.

I only ate half of the tart and threw the rest of it away later."

I brightened. "Well, good! That was a step in the right direction."

"No. I want to win this battle against food once for all. Throwing away half a tart – full of sugar and wheat, both things I shouldn't eat – isn't winning."

"But it _is_! You have to start somewhere to begin gaining victory." *Why did my Katrina seem so far away? Where was she going?*

"It's going to take so long if I do it that way, though, Heidi. I don't want to struggle with this forever."

"You won't, as long as you begin to believe that your battle can be won a step at a time. If you give up because you're waiting to throw all your efforts into a big showdown against temptation, you'll lose. You know that."

"I know, I know." She was done talking. I swallowed my last sob at the look on Katrina's face. There was no use going on. I'd said what I wanted to say and could only hope that God would give Katrina the help from it that she needed. Maybe I shouldn't bring up the subject again; our sister bond seemed less strained when I left the food issue alone.

•   •   •

Right after coming home from Summit, Katrina turned her energy to preparing for a short-term mission trip to the Philippines. Daddy was excited that one of his kids was finally going to the same country where, long ago, he had spent ten months that profoundly impacted his life.

" – it changed me in so many ways," Daddy's voice finally broke into her thoughts. "I'm grateful you have this chance to go to a third-world country and experience some of what I did." He smiled and rubbed her shoulders. She relaxed, soaking up the love in his touch. Daddy always gave her a sense of safety in the midst of unsettling changes. She listened quietly as he kept telling memories of his own trip to the Philippines.

After he gave her shoulders a last squeeze and left, she turned back to the computer and finished writing a thank you letter to one of her supporters.

Life-changing? Spiritual high? She didn't really believe that what Daddy was saying would ever happen to her.

86

Yet the letters went out, the money came in, and Katrina matter-of-factly faced the prospect of sweating out the summer in the Philippines.

Her mission team was assigned to work at a place called Camp Bato where they spent eight weeks building a concrete dormitory. Food was not as big an enemy for Katrina, since the team ate mainly rice, vegetables, fruit, and some meat. Instead, mosquitoes, oppressive humidity, primitive living conditions, and bonding with very different teammates presented plenty of immediate challenges to deal with.

During her team debriefing, a time of evaluating the missions experience and preparing to re-enter first-world living, Katrina jotted down some painfully honest thoughts about the future. She called God's perfect plan for her "the Promised Land," which she knew from past experience was full of mountains and giants to conquer: gluttony, being too busy for devotions, lack of desire to grow close to God, lack of willpower to get things done, fear of conversation with others, pride in looking good, jealousy of others, and a critical spirit. She zeroed in on these mountains that she needed to climb, but didn't look very closely at the One strong enough to help her reach the summits.

At the end of her trip, Katrina admitted, "Somehow I have a vague feeling that my life should be different because of this trip. I don't think anything has happened to me. I would like to begin to follow Jesus more closely at some point. It is hard to renounce the world for Jesus' sake... the pleasures of the world are too big in my life."

When she came back, browner than normal, she was unusually expressive and full of stories. I wondered what the experience did for her spiritual life, but I had to wait to find that out. The day Katrina arrived home, we sat cross-legged on the floor and enjoyed her animated show-and-tell. She drew us in to Filipino life with lively, often funny descriptions; her word-pictures made us hungry to hear more.

"Katrina," Rachel asked, "how'd you get this coconut and knife through customs? Isn't that illegal?"

She grinned slyly. "Well, kind of, but the customs man never asked about them. I wrapped them up in some clothes and stuck them in the bottom of my duffel bag."

"What's this called?" David said, holding up a piece of fabric.

"I don't remember, actually, but it has a lot of uses – as a skirt, a curtain, whatever you want. That reminds me of the day one of my teammates and I went to the market to look for this fabric…" and she was off into another story.

•   •   •

We were all home for a week. It was the last time our whole family would be together.

We had a siblings' sleepover, which involved lame wisecracks, a lot of laughing and popcorn and, of course, little sleep. Another night, we cranked up the volume on some patriotic band music, set off fireworks on the lawn, and took turns trying to chop open Katrina's coconut with David's machete. (You do what you must to create entertainment when you're forty minutes from the nearest town.) We sometimes crammed into the grain truck with David and rumbled out to the field to get a load of wheat from the harvesting combines. There's a video clip of us dancing to some country song on the truck radio, with Katrina holding ladylike reserve in the background. She was smiling, though.

During that week, we had one of those sweltering days that makes a person feel like trying something dumb.

"We need exercise," Katrina said, breaking up our talk in the warm schoolroom. She gathered up her Philippines photos, and put them back in their envelopes.

I yawned. Rebecca groaned and rested her head on her desk. "I don't wanna go anywhere," she said.

I poked her in the ribs, and she giggled, jerking upright. "Come on, you heard what Katrina said. Let's go."

We walked side by side, past the grain storage bins, up over the hill and down beyond the cliff to the creek. Our arms brushed against each other sometimes, and other times I'd reach over and tickle Rebecca, just to hear her shriek. How good it felt to have my sisters beside me.

"Tell us more about the Philippines," Rebecca said.

"What do you want to know?" Katrina answered as she knelt down to pick wild oat barbs out of her socks. Rebecca and I lazily watched.

"Tell us about snorkeling," I said. Katrina stood up and we kept walking.

"Well, we went down to this place called Moalboal Beach –"

88

"Weird name," Rebecca said.

"Yeah, I don't know what it meant. Anyway, this was where I found all the shells that I brought home. It was *so* gorgeous there! The water went out, brilliant blue as far as you could see," she gestured toward the snow-capped mountains far out in front of us, "and for the first few feet, I didn't see anything but shells. I thought it'd be a boring snorkeling experience. Then I went out into deeper water – far enough out that I saw the sandy bottom drop off into nothing."

"Ooohh, I'd hate that," I shivered.

"I think it was like the shelf I read about in science. Totally different species live out beyond the shelf in even deeper waters. Just beyond the shelf, I saw the most breathtaking thing – a school of fish, hanging as if they were suspended in the murky water. Flashes of silver came from some fish as they drifted along."

Katrina got more enthusiastic as she talked. "It's hard to even start describing it in words – it was so beautiful. You know those underwater pictures you see in *National Geographic* of tropical fish? Well, that's what I saw: brightly colored fish and coral below me. It was a *whole* lot better than what Rachel saw when she went snorkeling in Israel. Some fish had blue and yellow stripes, while others were an almost neon orange. You'd have liked them, Heidi. It was *amazing*."

"Didn't you worry about stepping on the coral?"

"Not really. I was wearing some old water shoes so whenever I stepped anywhere, the coral wouldn't scrape me. It's really rough and the ends are very sharp. There was more fine sand than coral, anyway."

"Did you build a sand castle on the beach?" Rebecca asked. "I mean, like that big one you made in California last year?"

"I started to, but we had to leave to go back to Camp Bato."

By now, we were at the creek, and we plopped down on the sharp, coral-like prairie grass to peel off our shoes and socks. The sun blazed at us. Rebecca was the first to stand on our footbridge plank, and like a ballerina, dip her toes in the water.

"Eww. It is so poop-itated," she complained. The cows had evidently been in and out of this one scarce source of water all summer.

"Be thankful for it," I said. "It's all we've got to cool off in." I stepped out onto the warm, silver-weathered wood and rocked back and forth, throwing Rebecca off-balance.

89

"Hey!" she squealed. "You made me almost fall into that gross water." She pushed me. Laughing, I pushed back. We both squealed. Katrina smiled quietly at us.

"How many can we fit on there?" she asked.

"Two is company, three's a crowd," I said. "Come on board and crowd us out."

Lapsing into companionable silence, we all sat down, swishing our bare legs and feet in the brown water.

"Ahhh."

"This is nice."

"Mmm-hmm."

A mile off, a grain truck went rumbling out toward the field to pick up a load of wheat. The air was full of snappings – dry seeds and grasshoppers on the move. Katrina leaned back as far as she dared on the narrow plank and looked up at the sky. "I liked the Philippines, but home is so much better," she said.

"Yeah, I bet."

More silence.

"It's hot out here," Rebecca said.

"Du-uh. What was your first clue?" I jabbed her.

She stood up and stared at the water's glittering surface. "You know, I wouldn't mind jumping in."

"So – do it!" We looked at her expectantly.

"In fact, I'm not at all afraid of jumping in," she said in a what-do-you-think-of-*that* tone. Just in case anybody had doubts.

"I dare you," I said.

"Me, too," Katrina chimed.

"What'll you pay me?" She grinned impishly.

"Hey, I thought that you weren't afraid. Now show us you aren't and do it without any payback," I said.

"I might, and I might not. I just want to know if you'll pay me."

"How about fifty cents?" I said.

"Ha! As if."

Around and around we went. By a series of coaxing, pleadings, and threatening, we all got wet. Somehow I was the first. I fell backward off the plank into water that had a whole lot of frigid, creepy mud underneath. Katrina and Rebecca shouted with laughter at the horrified expression on my face.

"Get me out, get me out!" I shrieked. They laughed so hard that it took a while for them to reach down helping hands to fish me out. Rebecca went in next and came up screaming.

"See?" I choked between roars of laughter.

"Oh, it's awful!"

Katrina walked off the plank. "Hey, where are you going? You're next," we said.

"I know," she answered. Sedately, she went to the edge of the pool that spread out under the footbridge and waded in until the water reached her waist.

"She's smart," Rebecca said, splashing herself to get the mud off. Katrina smiled, turned around and waded back out.

"There. I'm wet," she said. Her twinkling blue eyes were the color of her sopping T-shirt.

"Okay, okay, so you beat us in the brains category!" I smiled back. Being a threesome again felt so good.

•   •   •

I remember one of the last nights Katrina and I had together. While the light from Daddy's office shone across the hall into my bedroom, we talked late. I knew I was losing some of my closeness to Katrina. We kept the conversation light for a while, talking about her mission trip teammates.

"A couple of them were nice," Katrina said, "but I thought the rest of the girls were pretty immature."

"And Jim was kind of an attention-getter, huh?"

"Yeah. That's why he and Hailey got along so well – they had the same goal: attention."

I snickered, then assumed a tone of mock severity, "Naughty, naughty, Katrina. You really shouldn't be so – "

"Truthful?"

"Harsh, maybe. Whatever."

My mind was on another track. "Katrina, do you think you grew closer to God while you were over there?"

"No, not really." I heard her roll over in bed so that she was facing me.

"How come?"

She answered, "It's not that I didn't try to please God and be like Him. I guess I just didn't – "

"*Want* to grow closer?" I finished for her.

"Yeah."

"Why don't you want to?" I asked, worried.

91

After a moment of quiet, Katrina offered, "Probably because it seems like more work than reward."

"How so?"

"Well, because I know God calls us to sacrifice a lot, and to live a life that goes against everything we naturally want and *are*, as humans. I've thought a lot about this in regard to my struggles with food. I don't like the picture of dealing a deathblow to my bad habits every single day for who knows how long. In the Philippines, I wrote out some of the battles I'd have ahead of me. You know most of them."

I nodded, and then remembered she couldn't see my nod in the dark. "Ummm, yeah."

"I would like to win these," she said, "but it is too hard for me, or I don't really want to because I have one foot in the world and one foot in heaven. So because I have no motivation to get it together, I can't really set goals because they won't be accomplished."

I started to say something, but Katrina went on, "I know – I know that there are blessings, but it seems like all I can see are the sacrifices. I'm lazy. I don't want to wake up to a battle against myself every day for the rest of my life. There isn't a whole lot of appeal in that."

"You just admitted that there are blessings in living to please God, though!"

"Admitting isn't the same as doing. The Christian Filipinos are so happy, because their riches are in heaven. Mine are on earth."

"You can begin to put them in heaven! Nobody is saying that you're doomed – except you."

Silence.

"Which book is it," I said, "where Jesus says that we'll receive thirty, sixty or a hundred times more back what we have given up, not only in heaven, but also now?"

"I don't know."

"Oh well, it doesn't matter where the verse is. But think about that, Katrina. It's soooo awesome. So awesome! It's the hardest thing to die to ourselves like He asks, but when we do, we are so much more fulfilled. We have purpose to live! Don't you want that?"

"It costs a lot."

"But don't you want to make your addiction to food die? Don't you want to be free of it?"

92

"Yes, I do. I also know, from what Mama's given me to read about it, that it usually takes a long time to go back to normal eating habits – "

"Yeah, but – "

Katrina carried on her thought, "I have other bad habits, too, that I want to get rid of, but at the same time, I like them. I get a little pleasure out of doing what my flesh wants to do."

What to say to that? She was right. *Lord, what should I say?*

"Heidi, I see you – and Rebecca – finding that fulfillment in living God's way. I respect you so much for that. But when I watch you mature in Christ, I honestly don't long to be in the place you are. I just don't. There isn't a deep desire to grow close to God. I don't think it's right to be a hypocrite and walk the walk when my heart isn't in it."

A darkness in her tone made me want to cry. Before I knew it, the tears were rolling down my face. I sniffled quietly.

"Heidi? Are you crying?" Katrina sat up in bed. "Please don't cry for me," she said.

I gulped and squeaked out, "Katrina, I love you so much, and that's why it hurts to hear you say this. I long to see you happy."

I rolled out of bed and, kneeling beside Katrina's bed, reached out and put my arms around her. She held me close, and said regretfully, "I wish my struggles didn't have to affect you at all. I'm sorry."

"No, no," I pulled back and wiped my face on my pajama sleeve. "Don't think that at all! I *want* to help you. I *want* to bear your burden with you. You're so special to me, Katrina, and I want to do whatever I can to get you through this. Sometimes, though, I just don't know how to help."

"Keep on praying, I guess." She sighed heavily.

"Can we, now?"

"Sure."

Dear Heidi and Rebecca,

I love you two! And I'll miss you this fall. But the way time flies, I'll soon be home again for Christmas, and we'll have a few weeks to be together. Heidi, thank you for that heart-to-heart talk a few nights ago. I need someone to ask probing questions like that now and then.

93

A few days later, we stood shivering in the early morning air, waving goodbye to Katrina and Mama as they left for the airport. I still picture her, tall and tanned, wearing her black Philippines T-shirt, smiling sweetly. That was the last time we saw her alive.

Eight

Collapsing Towers
Taylor University - final semester

Katrina settled back into college life, this time in a different dorm room with a new roommate, Tiffany. She spent hours practicing and teaching piano, learning German in one class and ethnic dances in another, writing art analysis papers and perfecting several oil paintings for class. Although she was often frustrated by her inability to get painting and music right the first time, she still enjoyed being immersed in two things she really loved. She kept a smile ready for students she passed on campus sidewalks or in the dining commons. Girls in Katrina's dorm occasionally found thoughtful, encouraging notes from her on their doors.

Her emails to us were less than half of what they were the year before - mostly businesslike, taking care of school-related details. She was polite, but distant.

On September 11, we received our first truly heart-felt message from her.

Dear ones,

Wow. I can't believe today. It was just another usual day, I thought, when I crawled out of bed this morning. Went to my 8:00 class, then to the fitness center for an hour of exercise. When I saw what the newscasters were talking about on the TV's in the workout room, I was shocked. The World Trade Center had been attacked by a hijacked airplane full of passengers! During that hour, more planes crashed and the nationwide frenzy only increased. Everyone in the room watched in disbelief as they distractedly tried to exercise and comprehend the tragedy at the same time. It's incredible. The whole Taylor campus is overtaken by the event, and it's the subject of conversations everywhere.

So many dead. The numbers aren't determined yet, but they'll be in the thousands, I'm sure. In the Pentagon alone, there are 23,000 workers, and in each World Trade tower, at least 10,000 workers. On TV, I saw live video footage of people throwing themselves out of the Twin Tower windows, flailing hundreds of feet to the ground. I suppose they were so desperate to avoid being crushed in the collapsing towers that they just tried to get away from it all...

Love,
Katrina

Katrina was becoming desperate to avoid being crushed by something, too. Internet pornography bore down on her soul. We don't know exactly when she got lured into online images, or how she got around the protective software filters installed by the university. I assume it began that fall, but it could have begun earlier.

Like anyone else who has been lured into pornography, Katrina kept her struggle hidden. She never talked to us about this additional burden hanging around her neck, relentlessly pulling her down. A month before she committed suicide, Katrina's guilt and desperation spilled out in writing. We came across it after she died.

"So, Katrina," her conscience began, "tell me about how you're feeling right now."

"It's pretty obvious, isn't it?" Katrina replied. "Long face, short remarks. I've just been doing something that I know grieves God. I've looked at porn on the Internet, and have eaten bad stuff today. I even skipped dinner because I've eaten 800 calories' worth of pop tarts. But then this evening I went and bought almost two dollars worth of pop tarts and stuffed myself on them till I felt kind of sick."

Conscience: "So with the porn you're ruining your mind, and with the food you're ruining your body."

Katrina: "Yeah, that's about it."

"How can you be so matter-of-fact about this? Doesn't it concern you that you're doing these things? Aren't you worried about future consequences of what you're doing?"

"I suppose I am, but the lust of these things draws me to them even when something inside me says, 'no, don't do that.' It's a cycle – I do something wrong, feel guilty about it, confess it to God, and sooner or later, do the same thing again. It doesn't end."

"How about other people in your life? The things you do affect them, too. You know that."

"I know that, yes. And it's partly because of them that I feel guilty and try to stop my sins. I don't like to think what my family

96

would say if they knew what I feast my eyes on on the Internet. They'd probably take away my computer and give me a serious talking-to. They already know about the food issue, and that concerns them and probably will continue to until I can confidently say that I've gotten victory over it."

"Wow. I never realized you were such a sinner. What with the life you've had – good family, attending church every Sunday, and going to a good Christian college – I would never have imagined that you could possibly fall into these sins. It's as if you purposely went and looked for ways to sin."

"Well, the food thing wasn't exactly intentional. It grew gradually until it consumed me. The porn, on the other hand, was something I think I started to look for. It's addictive, like everybody says it is. How stupid of me not to have stayed away from this pit of quicksand."

"But then, you act stupid a lot of times."

"Shut up! You're not helping me any."

"Well, as I always say, the ignorant don't realize their sin, and so they need people like me to help them out."

"But I do realize my sin."

"You're sure not trying to get rid of it."

"Do you know how incredibly hard that is? I've battled this food issue for almost two whole years, and it's not getting any easier. Sometimes I think I'm winning, and sometimes I think someone else is winning."

"Sounds as though you're not a very happy camper."

"Huh. That's pretty perceptive of you. I try to cover up these sins and struggles so that other people will think I'm a normal friendly human being whose only problems consist of things like burnt toast and dead car batteries. It's hard, sometimes, to behave 'normally,' because I'm so out-of-whack inside that I have to actually think twice before I know what would be an appropriate action, and what would not. When I watch other people, their social behavior is much more fluid and natural than mine feels."

"I think you're making this a bigger deal than it deserves to be."

"Yeah, sometimes I think that, too. But I also think, 'anything that distances me from God and friends is a big deal.' And

I do want to be able to associate comfortably with people."

"So explain to me exactly why you feel you can't do this."

"When my mind is littered with thoughts about people's private parts, or their sexual appeal (as a result of the porn I've looked at), it's very difficult to behave freely and in a friendly way with others. I'm always distracted by those sinful thoughts. And when some social event is going on, and there's food available, I'm distracted by the presence of the food, which, for me to eat it, would be sin. So I guess it's the distractions in my mind that make me feel awkward."

"Hm. That's hard. I'm not sure what to say..."

If Only You Knew
on pornography addiction

I want to wrap my arms around you and tell you that I still love you. I really do! I ache for you, that you couldn't see sexual intimacy as one of God's greatest gifts anymore.

Dear Katrina, *you weren't alone* in your struggle. I've had my own share of wrong thoughts about sex and the human body. So have many, many others. But miraculously, God offers to cleanse us of the ugliness within.

I remember in one of my last conversations with you at home, somehow the subject of sexual temptation and how to keep pure thoughts came up. I grieve that that was the only time we ever talked about it, and what little we did say that night was pretty hesitant and general. What has lingered in my memory isn't the specifics of the conversation so much as the great sense of relief I felt to find I was not alone in my temptations. Knowing you also were fighting the battle for pure thoughts, I was encouraged not to give in or give up.

As a single, very sheltered girl, I was pretty much ignorant of, but quite curious about, anatomy. Most of the time when I stumbled on any kind of male nudity (even an encyclopedia picture of Michelangelo's statue of the biblical David), I quickly flipped to the next page. Magazines in the check-out line mainly stirred mild curiosity in me, and sometimes aroused brief sexual desire, even though I didn't know then that that was what I was feeling. Yet for having been so protected, I often let my thoughts wander places that made me feel dirty. I created vague images about how I thought sex or others' bodies might look. I know, it seems impossible in our sex-saturated Western culture that I was so sheltered.

My thought life was partly fed by Christian romance novels. I started reading the genre when I was ten, and I clearly remember the first scene that hooked me, arousing greater curiosity and also sexual desire. There was plenty of material for my fertile imagination on the shelves of church libraries. Deep down, I knew what I was reading was wrong for me then, and I was secretive enough that Mama was unaware that my vast book diet included piles of romance novels. Now I know that things that cause me to choose isolation and deception, even seemingly innocent novels, are harmful for me. Maybe even an addiction.

I wish I had listened to Shannon Ethridge, "What is wrong for you now is anything that arouses sexual desire that cannot be legitimately fulfilled." And that can only be found in marriage.

You said you kind of fell into bulimia, but deliberately looked for pornography. I don't know what tipping point caused that, though I often think that your sense of worthlessness from being so entrenched in bulimia probably made you reason that since you were on your way down to the Land of Broken-Beyond-Repair, it couldn't hurt to distract yourself with more fleeting pleasure. I never saw your computer internet history, but I still wonder how you, my technically unsavvy sister, managed to skirt the university filters... and when you figured out how to, did you feel any hesitation? Any fear of what was to come?

Women addicted to pornography often feel like they are broken beyond repair in a sexually rabid culture that typifies men's pornography addiction as the only normal. According to the Education Database Online in 2011, "Of the 40 million Americans who regularly visit porn sites, 33% are women."

Crystal Renaud adds, "Seventeen percent of all women struggle with pornography addiction." Thankfully, people are becoming more aware that women struggle in this area too, and ministries and helps are arising for such women who used to feel completely alone.

Women who keep their addictions secret are driven further into despair because they have no support system to lift them out of the "pit of quicksand", as you called it. Renaud agrees, "The thing about living a life of deception...is that it promotes a life of isolation as well." This is the exact opposite of what God intended sexual pleasure to accomplish in our lives - not isolation, but communion

99

with another at the deepest level possible. He meant to draw together a husband and wife, each intrinsically selfish, and in the sexual act, not only give them physical pleasure, but also pleasure in meeting each other's needs, looking outside themselves to minister to each other.

I am so undeserving that in my marriage to Jesse, I have been given the whole beautiful picture of what sex really is. Yes, I meant *beautiful*. I can't think of a more delightful way for God to unite a man and woman – not just in body, but heart and soul, too.

You couldn't link "beautiful" to sex because you only saw a partial picture of it. There isn't any heart and soul in pornography, just strangers' naked bodies. When you developed an obsessive awareness of others' sexuality, you felt increasingly out of whack. Because you were. And porn addiction is. It is the powerfully twisted, seductive counterfeit of a gift from God.

God designed sex so that a man and woman could offer themselves completely to each other. It is a holy, sacrificial act. But pornography strips away the holiness and dresses sex in insatiable lust. As you discovered, human beings are reduced to a bunch of body parts intended for your personal viewing pleasure. The intimacy of sex is shattered by pornography. What is meant to be enjoyed between one man and one woman who are committed to each other for life suddenly becomes an ugly peepshow. Millions of men and women are gratified for a little while by staring at the body of a stranger. Then they look for something more stimulating to their senses.

Lust is a raging fire, seeking fuel to keep it alive. It is, said C.S. Lewis, "an ever increasing craving for an ever diminishing pleasure. . . . To get a man's soul and give him nothing in return– that's what really gladdens [Satan's] heart." From magazines in the checkout line to X-rated films, pornography's whole business strategy is to feed the fire of lust.

You gave up in hopelessness before you found ways to douse that fire. How could you have fought back?

After overcoming her own porn addiction, Crystal Renaud founded Dirty Girls, a ministry to other addicts. She focuses on the acronym SCARS in counseling women who are porn addicts:

S - "Surrender begins by asking the question, 'Do I trust God enough to get well?'" Part of learning to trust God to cleanse and restore us is learning to mistrust ourselves and the innate sinfulness of our hearts. We all have problems deeper than dead car batteries and burnt toast. And if we think we can just hold ourselves out of reach of sin, we are kidding ourselves to death.

C - "Confess your sins to each other and pray for each other so that you may be healed." (Jas. 5:16)

A - "Accountability restores the character that has been lost in us and makes us into women of integrity...something most of us have been living without for too long. We've told so many lies that we may not even trust ourselves anymore...'fools think their own way is right, but the wise listen to others.'" (Prov. 12:15, NLT)

Crystal encourages women to find accountability in a support group as well as in another woman who is more spiritually mature, preferably one who has struggled with porn addiction as well, but has been victorious over it for more than a year.

R - "By accepting responsibility, we begin looking less inside ourselves and more to the outside - where our actions...have had an impact on others...Create a personal inventory of how your addiction has harmed others. This step is about growing in maturity [, m]oving away from denial, blame or self-pity."

S - "Sharing [your] story is an essential part of healing...This...should be done after at least 6 weeks of freedom... You will need to share again and again, because we can never finish rejoicing in the work the Lord has done in us."

Katrina, being addicted to pornography didn't put you in a category of "too sinful" where God's forgiveness couldn't reach you! The God who created love and sex was right there with you in all those dark and wasted hours, at every click of the mouse, seeing those images on your screen. He didn't cut off His love for you! No, the Son of God was calling you, "Katrina, come back to me! Let me heal you. You are not so broken I cannot fix you. The Spirit of the Sovereign Lord... has sent me to proclaim that captives will be released and prisoners will be freed!" (Isa. 61:1, NLT)

Nine

My Heart Grows Faint
Taylor University - last days

God said, "I did not create you to abandon the ship of life when you encounter high seas and furious storms. I designed that you remain in your boat and have Jesus join you. Only then will the storms in your life be stilled." Albert Wedel, family friend

•　　•　　•

Oct. 3

Two weeks before her death, Katrina hands in an analysis of the play, "Death of a Salesman." She observes that "this modern-day tragedy seems to comment on the human inclination to live in illusion rather than reality... Willy Loman [the salesman] stands as a prime example of a life unfulfilled, a sobering reminder of the darker side of life."

The play ends abruptly with Willy's suicide.

Thursday, Oct 11

Katrina writes home,

I haven't been looking for a good plane fare lately, but I know I need to. Maybe this weekend I'll take some time for that.

I'm planning to visit Uncle Mike and Aunt Jo during fall break (Oct. 18-21).

Friday, Oct. 12

Katrina writes to Daddy and Mama,

I've been noticing a general I-don't-care attitude of mine lately, and I think it stems from a deep dissatisfaction I feel toward myself. This attitude of course affects everything negatively, and is robbing me of the proper interest I should have in my studies. I'm struggling to motivate myself and just *do it*! I'm starting to feel "behind" in my assignments and study, and this is a very uncomfortable realization for me. I hesitate to tell you these things because I know they discourage you, and I know what I must do to fix them, and I've gotten so much advice that I'd have to be a total moron to *not* know how to get it right. When something is wrong and you know the right thing to do but don't do it, that's called cowardice, isn't it?

Mama replies,

I sense a bit of discouragement in your email. That's very normal for all of us, and it's good that you can let us know about it. Let God know about it too - He cares. You are His child. Maybe you could read part of a Psalm each morning. One of my favorites is Psalm 121.

Much love to you and a big squeeeeeeeeeeze!

Daddy also replies,

You express some dissatisfaction. That is normal, Katrina. Life has those "dissatisfaction" times. Don't feel somehow responsible about it. Those times are hard to explain, but we all go through them now and then. I am sure they are engineered by God for good. Sometimes they last a long time, sometimes they last a short time... I think what God wants of us as we go through those times is a steadfast eye on Him and a trust that He knows what He is doing in our lives.

Love to you, schweetie.

Tuesday, Oct. 16

Nelson Rediger, who works at Taylor, writes Daddy and Mama, "Katrina is the greatest. She and a friend truly ministered to one of our 50th class reunion alums, Chuck, last week at homecoming. Here is what Chuck says: 'Loneliness is a reality with me since [my wife] Lynn died in April. Sitting alone in the dining commons prompted some tears until two students asked to sit at the table. It was fun talking with these students. They are fine, talented Christian ladies.'"

Wednesday, Oct. 17

Katrina's daytimer:
- Art as Experience paper due
- Call oxygen place to ask if they accept out of state checks; transfer $ from savings to checking account

- 5:30 haircut
- evening – call Jennie Lee – dinner with her Thurs, borrow car Fri morn, take car Thurs nite?

     The art paper Katrina turns in is about a Swedish film, "Wild Strawberries," which follows Isak Borg's lifetime of cold-heartedness and selfish choices to a surprising twist. "At age 78, Isak realizes how empty his life has been," Katrina writes poignantly, "despite its outward appearance of success, and he starts to change for the better."

     She asks dear elderly Jennie Lee, who lives by the university, if she could borrow her car to "run some errands," and Jennie regretfully says no, her insurance would not allow it. But she would be happy to get her friend to drive Katrina wherever she needed to go, would she like that?

     No, thank you, Katrina says. She wouldn't want to be a bother.

     She returns to school and asks another student Megan, who has loaned out her car to others.

     Sure, says Megan.

Thursday, Oct. 18 - 8:07 am

Dear family,

     It's a chilly but beautiful day today - bright sun and clear sky. The leaves are abundant on the grass and skittering everywhere along the sidewalks and parking lots. With so many people leaving for Fall Break, the campus is becoming pleasantly quiet, and I think I'll be able to get a lot done this weekend.

     I'm staying here on campus over the weekend. Yes, I managed to find a ride to South Bend, but it was almost last minute and would have required Aunt Jo to drive 45 minutes one way to pick me up. I just feel like enjoying a quiet, relaxing weekend here rather than in South Bend.

     Thanks for calling this morning, Mama. I hope you have a great trip to British Columbia and a good time with Grandpa Hamm and the other relatives. Enjoy your weekend!
With love,
Katrina

Katrina's daytimer:
- fall break begins after last class
- no piano pedagogy, no dance, no bell ringers
- reserve tank at Indiana Oxygen Co.?
- lunch at Grille
- get paycheck at cashier's office

Friday, Oct. 19 - 9:45 am
Dearest Katrina,

How's my girl? I'm sad that you weren't able to visit the Borns this weekend...It must be very quiet in the dorm. You should be able to finalize your Christmas travel plans this weekend.

Yesterday afternoon Rebecca came down with a sore throat...she doesn't feel well at all...Heidi is a good one for cheering her up. I was going to have them do impromptu talks this morning and had to postpone them because 50% of my class can't even talk!

What sorts of things are you doing this weekend? Did Pastor Thom ever reach you by phone?

Thankful for daily blessings and for you, my lovely daughter,
Love,
Mama

Friday - around 3 pm
Katrina sits at her dorm computer and types a letter of her own, then records herself reading the letter. The dorms are very quiet. Her roommate, Tiffany had already left around noon. Katrina seals the letter in an envelope, picks up her heavy backpack and walks down the hallway to another dorm room.

She knocks. "Megan?"

The door opens, and Megan steps out. Music and warm light floats past her to Katrina.

"Hey there, Katrina! I was just doing some homework. Oh, did you come for my car keys?" She disappears, comes back and tosses the keys to Katrina.

"Thank you. I really appreciate this."

"No problem! I'm glad I could help you out. I won't need the car till tomorrow night, anyway. Just fill it with gas, okay? The gas cap is kind of tricky to put back on. You have to wiggle it down just right."

106

Katrina nods. "Well, I should let you get back to studying. Thanks again, Megan," Katrina smiles and turns away.

"All right, see ya! Have a good time." Megan's door closes, cutting off the light and music.

Friday - 8:30 pm

The phone rings in Katrina's room. Jennie Lee is calling to see if Katrina found a car to use.

No one answers.

Friday - 9 pm

I sit alone in the schoolroom, typing a letter to Katrina. I figure she needs some Heidi-cheer and news from home.

I'm looking forward to this week away from home and school as a chance to have R & R and see what it's like. Being in British Columbia will be such a treat. Of course, I wish you were with us. But since you can't be, I'll tell you all about the trip when we get back, okay?

What's up with you? Is folk dancing still fun? And have you tried the maxixe? I love that word. It's so... sophisticated and smooth. What about painting? I haven't heard a peep about it, but I'd love to know. Do you wear a beret perched jauntily on your head, and adopt an extremely suave look and vigorously dash paint on three different canvases at once? ...Tell me what you're doing these days, okay? What's on your mind? What have you been enjoying lately? What are your thoughts on Taylor's campus life? Is studying difficult or have you found somebody to study with? I really do want to know.

Katrina hasn't been saying much lately, is clammed up about her eating habits, and I notice that her reserve even extends sometimes to what she is learning in class or doing over the weekend.

This is a hard thing, I think, *but if I really, truly wanted it all to change, I would be praying more earnestly and faithfully for her than I have been.*

I finish the letter, sign off with love, and hit the print button. Over the noise of the printer, I hear Mama calling from the kitchen,

107

"Heidi, are you going to bed?"

"Yes, ma'am, I yam, I yam." I smile, sealing the letter in an envelope.

Mama says with mock sternness, "Don't you call me that! I am your *muh*-ther, not 'ma'am.'"

"Oh, woops. Sorry!"

"Don't forget that you have to get up early tomorrow."

"I remember," I say, walking into the kitchen to give Mama a squeeze. "Sometimes I think I'm going to break one of your bones hugging you."

"Am I that fragile?" Mama plants her hands on her hips.

"No, you're just so thin – no, slender! I meant *slender*."

"Well, that's a nicer word than *thin*."

"Right," I say.

Mama hugs me tight. "Now off to bed with you."

I drop the letter in the mail slot on my way. There. That piece of news from home should cheer up Katrina-the-homebody.

Friday - around midnight

A campus security officer finds Megan's car parked on the far edge of campus, behind a science building. Within minutes, headlights, sirens, squealing brakes and the bang of car doors fill the place. Voices join other voices. A cold breeze blows past warm bodies standing, walking around, examining the car's interior.

The campus officer, Brad, stands back, watching. In shock. He has found something he never expected to see on his campus rounds.

A couple of people lift a limp form from the back seat and lay it on a gurney. Emergency medical techs draw the sheet up and slide the body into an ambulance. Police cars, lights flashing, follow the ambulance out of the parking lot. Their sirens are silent now. There is no need to hurry back to a hospital.

As the white procession pulls away, Brad glances down at the car. In the maroon upholstery of the backseat, he can see faint lines where her body was curled up. Her face flashes through his mind.

Nothing but a note on the back window is left – the tank, hose, mask, list of supplies, and her backpack were taken to the morgue. Brad tears her note off the window and reads it again, "Please be careful: helium fumes in the vehicle."

Streaks of light coming from the open car doors spill out

108

across the parking lot. Brad stares, mesmerized. When will her family find out? They are probably sleeping right now. He shakes his head incredulously. Time to get back to the campus safety building and file a report. But he has something else to do first. He walks around the car, closing all the doors and starts to pray for a family he's never met.

The sound of the slamming doors echoes through the black woods beyond.

Saturday, Oct. 20

A few hours later and almost two thousand miles away, two cars speed down a gravel road toward the farmhouse, dust billowing out behind them. The blue heeler, Tie, begins to bark in the chill light of dawn. He stands stiffly at the porch door, eyeing and sniffing the three people who step out onto the driveway. Two of them smell familiar.

Pastor Ron reaches his hand toward the dog, "Hey, boy, remember us? We were here last night for supper."

He looks down. His hand trembles, not for fear of Tie, who is now wriggling happily around his ankles, but for… something he has never encountered before. He shoves his hands in his pockets.

His wife Jean tugs at his jacket sleeve, and they follow Jeff, the police officer, into the porch, up the steps, and stand there before the door for a moment. Ron and Jean wait for Jeff to knock.

The thumping on the front door jolts Mama awake from a nightmare. Groggy, Daddy instinctively rolls out of bed and pulls his robe on.

"Who could that be?" Mama sits up, shaking the nightmare out of her head and staring at the clock. Five in the morning?

"I don't know." Wide awake now, Daddy hurries out of the room with Mama following close behind. She always worries about strange people coming to their house at odd hours.

The rustling of their robes and footsteps down the hallway wake me.

"Rebecca," I hiss. "Rebecca, wake up!"

She wakes up reluctantly. "What?" Her cold makes her voice croaky.

"Daddy and Mama are up. I wonder if they're getting ready for the trip."

"But they shouldn't be," Rebecca says, pointing to the alarm clock. "It's five o'clock. I thought that Daddy was going to sleep in

109

this morning, because he's not coming with us on our trip."

"Well, they're up. I think someone's here. Want to go see what's going on?" I try to keep my tone light, but somehow the room has grown tense.

"Maybe it's nothing," Rebecca says. "Maybe someone's lost and asking for directions."

Just as Rebecca's words begin to settle the thumping I feel inside, both of us hear voices and the creaking of the entryway floor. Funny. Daddy doesn't normally invite anyone into the house to give them directions on how to get back to the nearby highway. We sit up in our beds, trying to decide whether we should get up. The voices split up, some moving away toward the living room, and one coming toward our bedroom.

"Russ, I'm going to get the girls up. I think they need to be there with us." Mama's whisper sharpens as she approaches our door. Mama could never seem to get the hang of whispering softly; she always pronounces her "s" too sharply.

And when she's upset, it gets worse, I think.

She flutters in, leaf-like, wearing her old pink housecoat. She says something. We get up, make ourselves presentable, hurry down the hallway, and turn the corner into the living room.

We are so completely unprepared.

Nothing will register properly. My stare flies from Jeff's brown uniform to Ron and Jean and back again.

A police officer? Did Rachel get hurt in Brazil? Is that why they're all here? Oh, goodness, I bet she did something stupid being adventurous like she is...

This is bizarre.

And why are Ron and Jean back? They were just over last night.

I shiver. I can't stop staring.

Daddy sits at one end of the couch next to me, his hair all mussed up, the smile gone from his eyes. He leans forward intently. On the other side of him, Rebecca holds a princess-like posture, knees together. And beyond her, Mama trembles.

Is somebody going to hurry up and tell us what happened to Rachel?

Jeff clears his throat, shuffles on the rug.

"I'm... I'm sorry to say this, but your daughter, Katrina, died last night."

Everything freezes for a split second -

- and then completely falls apart.

I almost hear the pieces shattering around me, and start to cry because he isn't lying and I know it.

Jeff's face is so serious. And sad. *Why is he sad?*

Oh, he said Katrina died.

What? Was it a car accident? Was she riding with someone when they crashed and she died while we were sleeping last night? Oh, God.

"Oh, God," I cry it into my hands, and the tears drip on my feet. So cold.

Mama weeps deep, awful cries. Rebecca puts her arm around Mama's quivering shoulders, and the tears run quietly down her face. I look at her calmly, but not.

Daddy alone sits rigidly aloof. He is waiting for something.

Mama looks at Pastor Ron. Surely our spiritual shepherd, our nice pastor, will correct the awful mistake.

She screams the words inside, but he only hears a hoarse whisper, "What happened?"

"It was suicide," he says gently.

"Noooo!" Mama wails.

Ron shrinks into his chair, looking like someone kicked the air out of him. He lets Jeff take over, whose jumbled words pound thick and heavy into our heads.

"A university security guard found her body... call from local police... researched this carefully, and knew exactly what she was doing – "

"How did she – " Daddy begins. I stare at him in fear. His face is a deadpan mask, and there are no tears.

Mama breaks in, choking out between sobs, "Where did, where did – she find out how to do – this?"

"She looked on the Internet. There are a lot of sites that explain how you can take your life. Like I said, she researched it carefully, and found out everything she needed to know to make sure it was successful."

"Upland police found a list of supplies in her car. She had rented a tank of helium in Marion and hooked it up to a hose connected to a mask that she placed over her face. Eventually she ran out of oxygen."

No oxygen. She is dead? She is dead?

When you run out of oxygen, you're dead, right? Can't the police have got it wrong?

111

"Well, she, uh … left a letter for you… found it in her backpack…" Jeff looks at the four of us going into shock.

Daddy shakes himself upright, his back ramrod straight. "Where is she?"

"Her body was taken to the county morgue, where the coroner performed an autopsy. The body will have to be embalmed today."

I shudder, retching.

"Authorities there are transporting the body back here by plane in the next day or two." Jeff stops. "I'm so sorry. I wish I didn't have to tell you these things. I just want you to know that my condolences are with you, and I want to help you however I can."

Daddy has broken down. His grief is louder than Jeff's words.

My dearest family – Daddy, Mama, Rachel, David, Heidi, and Rebecca,

First let me say that I love each of you and that I look forward to you joining me in heaven. I'm sure it's a beautiful place, and everyone is happy there.

You're probably asking "Why?" right now, so I'll attempt to answer you. The reason I decided to take my life is that I can no longer deal with the struggles in my life. I've tried so many times to "get it right" with my outer and inner self, but I just can't (or won't). Many methods and tactics – including Biblical ones – have been used in their turn, but none have worked for me. Temptations continually provoke me into doing wrong, other people's actions annoy me, my daily prayer/Bible-study time is either dry or non-existent, I am full of impure thoughts…

Some things of the future look hard. I fear some of its many challenges – tough college assignments, possibly marriage and raising children, old age with its arthritis and health problems (believe me, I've cracked my joints enough that I'm guaranteed to suffer with arthritis someday). I don't want to grow old. I'm nineteen years old and already I have many regrets about the past. "Regretting the past and fearing the future…"

You know about my eating difficulties. I think that is the hardest thing right now for me. It constantly distracts me, gets in my way, tempts me. I've battled it for two years, and the strain tires

112

me. I'm just tired. I know I'm not eating right, I fear becoming fat because of this, my mind is habituated to thinking about food, and I just cannot or will not fix the problem. I've subconsciously allowed the Food Idol to be the commanding force of my life, causing me to order my days around it. I suppose I'm quite self-centered and selfish.

Another developing addiction is pornography. If bulimia/gluttony was my first attempt at finding a pleasure outlet in my busy life, then pornography is becoming the second attempt. I find things on the Internet and waste hours filling my mind with trash. This trash pollutes my mind, of course, robbing me of any innocence and causing uncomfortable thoughts to pop into my head at awkward social moments. I didn't think this was an addiction when I first started, and I still don't, but it certainly draws me to it. Those computer images stay in my mind and make me feel guilty when I sing, "Purify my heart" in church. I can't worship wholeheartedly anymore. My heart is calloused and cold and I don't care anymore. Naturally, when I am so engrossed with myself in the present moment, I don't invest in the future very well. My responsibilities are getting done later and later, and with less care.

Our family is very fortunate compared to many other families. We are all Christians, we love each other, we encourage and support one another. A lot of people don't have it as good as we do. And that's something that you'll probably puzzle over: why did I do this if I had it so good? What is it that I'm trying to get away from or solve by taking my life? Certainly not my family situation, because it's the most positive part of my life. And please don't blame yourselves for *anything*. It is all my fault, for not taking responsibility for my actions and for bringing an end to everything. I don't want anyone who has ever had anything to do with me to blame themselves in any way.

I know. I have researched suicide on the Internet and I am not ignorant of its symptoms, its procedures, and its results. Yet I feel that it is best. I am tired and I just want to sleep forever. We humans were created not for a brief life on Earth, but for eternal life either with or without God. I am going to leave, and how I look forward to it!

I brought the end upon myself the best way I knew how. It

113

was quick, painless, easy, and clean — I just fell asleep and never woke up. Hopefully this makes it easier for you to deal with it. This wasn't my first attempt; I tried three times to take my life before succeeding. The first two times were by slashing my wrists, but I didn't cut deeply enough. The third time, I borrowed Tiffany's car and ran a hose from the exhaust pipe to the airtight window, but after idling the car for two hours, nothing happened. So I found something more effective.

You are welcome to read my computer-printed journal, in the folder beneath my bed. It contains a bit more info about all this.

Forgive me for not measuring up to your hopes and expectations. You worked hard to bring me up to be pleasing to God, and you always said you were proud of me. Thank you so much for your loving affirmations, and please know that I didn't do this to retaliate for anything you've done. I love you and want you to keep on with life, doing what you did before. I am glad to remove my pessimistic personality and my perpetual problems from your midst — I often sulked and wept and complained about my struggles and I'm sure you got tired of this. Please try to move on with life. I simply want to remove myself from the ranks of living people, and the last thing I want to do is drag down others with me.

How I desire to be free of my tiresome fetters, to live freely and joyfully with Jesus, never to experience sorrow again. Heaven awaits me.

I'm sorry you have to take care of everything for me — the bank accounts, the college financial things, all the cleaning-up and sorting through. But it's easier to do these things now rather than after a lifetime of amassing possessions.

God bless you and give you peace.
With all my love, Katrina

After the others leave, our little family just sits in the living room, must be for an hour, and cry. Finally, I have to get out of there.

I just have to go somewhere else. Maybe I can walk this off. Maybe, but only if my legs could hold me up; they don't seem to want to. My body is on its own now.

I pause at the outgoing mail slot, where my letter for Katrina sticks out. When did I put it in? Last night, I think, but am not sure

114

anymore. I pull it out. I ache all over. It hurts deep in my chest.

My body takes me down the hallway into the schoolroom. *Oh, Katrina,* I moan inside, leaning against the doorframe. *You spent hours in here with me... remember doing biology and reading me bits of literature? You're still going to come home at Christmas and keep Rebecca and me company, right?*

"See you at Christmas," you said. But you lied! You lied to all of us! How could you –

"Heidi?" Rebecca shuffles in, her face streaked with tears. She is all red around the eyes, but her golden hair tumbles over her shoulders and down her back, just like it does every other morning. How can she look normal but not, at the same time?

I find that in the midst of thinking, my body sat down on the chair by my desk. Heavily, Rebecca sits, too. We stare at each other. I don't know what to do or say. I pick up my Bible from the desk, and open it. Psalm 61.

"Should I read out loud," I ask.

"Yes, please," she says, the tears running silently down her cheeks.

"Hear my cry, O God; listen to my prayer. From the ends of the earth I call to you, I call as my heart grows faint; lead me to the rock that is higher than I."

I sob. How does God know we need this? "For you - you have been my refuge, a strong tower against the foe. I long to dwell in your tent forever and take refuge in the shelter of your wings..."

With Rebecca listening, I read on and on. I feel like I can't stop. Every word is new, and written for us. There, in the little fragile sanctuary of the schoolroom, I feel God's hands holding us and the pieces of our shattered world.

•   •   •

Weeping is the sound of a soul writhing in agony. To hear someone else weeping is to writhe, too. That's how it is hearing Mama from her bedroom. Rebecca and I rush out of the schoolroom, in our shock terrified that some other horrible news has come right on the heels of our sister's death. Mama is kneeling at the foot of her bed, her face buried in the bedspread, tears soaking the flowered pattern.

"Lord, why did you let my daughter go? I gave –" She chokes. "I gave birth to her." Anger and pity shoots through me as I

115

watch Mama's slender shoulders shake helplessly. What did she ever do to deserve this? It seems like she'll never stop. Why should she?

Flesh of her flesh is dead.

That big-eyed, irresistible girl-baby sucking at her breast. Soft skin. Low, childish tones, "My name is Gu-treena." Little head on her knee, "Mama, I'm having such troubles."

Oh little girl, little girl, your troubles are all gone and they took you, too. You've broken your mother's heart.

•   •   •

Eventually we sit down at the dining room table and I watch the sun come up, knowing Katrina can't see it, over there in Indiana.

Uncle Stan is the first person to come after Ron, Jean, and Jeff leave. He is weeping – Uncle Stan, of all people. I've never seen him cry before, this strong brother of Daddy. He is the gruff farmer, loving his kids tough and everyone else at arm's length. He comes to me, hugs me close and says, "I love you." It is the only time I hear him say that, and it brings more sobs as he holds me. He is such a silent man. Sitting in a corner chair, mostly staring out the window, waiting for a moment to help, he is a strangely comforting rock for us that whole day while we ache and wander the house and spill tears in soup that Mama makes us eat.

I take a nap because my head aches. I wake to the surreal world of a dead sister and a house full of grieving people. My cousin and his wife show up with arms full of Kleenex boxes. They let me hold their baby girl; her sweet innocence soothes. I am glad for her soft, trusting warmth and the fact that she listens, but doesn't talk. Talking is exhausting.

Lots of hugging and conversations I forget even before they are over. The living room crowds with people, some relatives and many people I didn't expect to show up. I pull out photo albums for them to thumb through, dazed. And always, in the corner, Uncle Stan sitting silently.

Rebecca answers the phone that won't stop ringing. I stay away from it. We get so many calls that we can't keep up writing the name of each caller in our phone notebook. Somebody finally scribbles, "and many more." The governor of Montana calls, the president of Taylor University calls; Daddy is so upset he almost doesn't speak to him. He is barely civil when he does pick up. His father-heart is broken that he wasn't there to protect his girl from

116

herself. He is angry at Taylor, believing they failed his beloved daughter.

Somebody brings food, but it turns my stomach. Briefly, I have an overwhelming desire to starve. My best friend is dead, anyway, so why not?

•   •   •

That night, in the office, I lean my aching head on my hand, resting my elbow on a stack of papers by the computer and help Daddy think of people to whom we should send the email with the subject line, "Katrina." Daddy writes, while I remind him of details he keeps forgetting. It tears me up inside, how helpless and confused he and Mama are.

I look at the top of his monitor and see a paper I stuck there years ago. No, wait, I did that yesterday. Daddy wasn't going to go with us on our trip to British Columbia, so the day before, I wrote a cheerful "we love you" note for him to look at while we were gone. My puffy eyes pass slowly over each signature on that note. Katrina's isn't there. I knew that. Of course, it wouldn't be. Katrina is away at college; that's why she didn't sign it.

Katrina "isn't" any more. She "was." I cry. Katrina will never sign anything again. Daddy will never hear her say "I love you" again in real.

The email comes out so calm in tone, even though Daddy is a wreck and "calm" is a state we pass in and out of as fast as the tears fall.

Dear Friend,

I am sorry for this impersonal e-mail. We need to get this message out to a lot of people in a short time and I chose this route.

Our dear Katrina, 19 years old, died last night. She was at college in Indiana at the time. We are still going through the emotions and struggles with the reality of this final situation. At the age of 7 she asked her mother if she could sing in church the song, "I Want to See My Savior First of All." She is now experiencing the full, glorious reality of that heart's desire. For that we rejoice. And we know as King David did so many years ago in Israel that we shall go to her but she cannot return to us.

We ask for prayer that somehow through this whole

117

experience, God will be magnified in our lives. We don't understand the depth of God's mind or the inexhaustible source of His love. He has made it clear that His ways are not ours nor are His thoughts ours. So we simply trust Him through this time. Will you trust with us? This brings things into perspective very clearly. I pray eternity is clearly fixed in your mind and that you have made things right with God – on His terms.

The date we chose for the service is October 25 – next Thursday at 3:00 pm... I assure you that though we would love to see you, hold you, and cry with you, we do not expect you here. We would appreciate the comfort your presence would provide for us, but we understand how difficult it may be to come this far. Your prayer for us is a wonderful alternative and we covet that especially now through Thursday... and beyond.

... Thank you for being there as our friends. We are so grateful that you are there for us during this our valley of the shadow of death. He promised He would go with us through that valley and never promised He would remove us from it. (Psalm 23) It is just so good to know of your love.

God bless you,
Russ, Lora, Rachel, David, Heidi, Rebecca

Daddy's broad shoulders are bent and shaking again as he types our names and pauses between *David* and *Heidi*, where *Katrina* should be. Warm tears flood my sore eyes. I put my hand on Daddy's shoulder, and look away from the now-blurry screen.

If Only You Knew
on suicide and survivor pain

Katrina, how could you just go, leaving me behind for the rest of my life – did you hear me – the rest of *my life*? I miss you *so* much. I hate it that I'm left to tell a story about someone I'm beginning to forget.

And you died. Oh God, you died. It's been over ten years, but sometimes I still shake with sobs for us and for you and the life you might have had if you had walked down that first path instead.

"Suicide is the simplest path," you told Daddy and Mama in the spring. Simplest for who? You? Or the thousands of people who

118

sorrowed that you left them in such an unfeeling way?

Who were you, really? The coroner said there was no evidence that you'd slit your wrists. You said you were falling behind in studies because of your pornography addiction, but university professors said you were working ahead. The journal under your dorm bed never turned up – you know, the one you said had more information about your choice to die. I don't understand how you thought you were being loving by hiding from us.

"I love you and want you to keep on with your life." I curse the demonic forces that got hold of you to make you write such a horrible thing in the name of love. That is not love. That is total blind hopelessness, not love. If you had even imagined, with that love for us, for one minute what our lives would be like after your death, would you have done it?

How could you not see how deeply we would suffer as we tried to move on? You made me weep when I was doing school and going to church, working at Bible camp, falling asleep at night, singing hymns, playing piano, celebrating birthdays, buying groceries, watching home videos and sunsets. The ache was unrelenting for so long.

You weren't at my high school graduation. I cried with the tassel hanging by my ear, not relieved at finally being done, but sad that you walked out on the celebration called Life. And when the tassel was flipped from one side of the mortarboard to the other, I had to walk ahead through life alone.

Okay, not completely alone. That's what it felt like sometimes, though I still had five people to call family. But you, Katrina, you were the middle one of us seven; you ripped a jagged hole in the center of our family.

The refrain that keeps on: "Katrina's gone." Everyday moments, noticing little details you would have loved and wanting to share them with you. Look at that miniature waterfall in the creek, Katrina. See the cats wrestling. Ha, ha, they look silly, don't they? You'll never guess what my kids said the other day...

Oh. You're not here.

And you're never coming back. Ever.

I want to scream – or hit something. I want to yell at you, Katrina. And then I want to cry until the stabbing ache is numbed. I feel helpless in the aftermath of a death I might have helped to prevent. I blame myself for not having more understanding when you did ask me for help. I just didn't see that the distress signals you sent out were so urgent. *How could I not see that?*

•　　　•　　　•

I am sad I only got seventeen years with my Katrina. But how much more tragic that she never lived out the sixty or seventy additional years she might have had! It is not just my loss, but the world's. We will never know all the ways God planned to use her life to impact others.

I think suicide is the choice of a mind completely confused by lies from Satan. It is selfishness repackaged by Satan to appear to the sufferer as the ultimate selfless step: *I'll just remove my problems from my family and friends' lives so I won't bother them anymore.* I think it is a tormented choice of escape that allows no room to truly consider how it would affect others.

Friend, maybe in your own despair, you are asking, "Why not suicide? Why not for Katrina? Or me?" She sidestepped a hard battle toward recovery, and went to a better place that was free of pain and temptation, right? If suicide solved her problems, why can't you walk that short, easy path, too?

Because it's not that easy or simple. Or short.

"If you are trying to kill yourself...the odds are against you," says one website. For every completed suicide, there are twenty-five failed suicides.

If you survive a suicide attempt, you could be mentally impaired, paralyzed, have organ damage, or lose one of your senses. A woman who shot herself in the head survived, but was blinded for the rest of her life. A man despairing of his gambling addiction survived a jump from a bridge, and is a paraplegic today. Failed attempts at the type of suicide Katrina chose can result in brain damage, as one woman shares, "A failed suicide attempt left me completely disabled, unable to work and with a severe hypoxic brain injury that affected many aspects of my life. I had to start from rock bottom and completely rebuild my entire life."

Beyond physical injury, there is incalculable emotional and psychological damage. Your relationships are strained because of fear, broken trust, anger, denial - you have come back to life on earth to find that you didn't just hurt yourself. You deeply wounded the people who love and care about you!

What if your attempt is successful?

My friend Kali found Mary, her roommate and close friend,

120

dead from a self-inflicted gunshot wound. You could still smell the gun smoke in her room, Kali said. "I think I found her maybe fifteen minutes after she shot herself." And there was another smell hovering, Kali remembers: the palpable sense of evil.

Mary had a broken past and struggled with depression; she talked a lot about both with Kali, and also shared some of her suicidal thoughts. Kali was there for her in every way possible, checking in on her often, asking how she was. But right before she died, Mary subtly became more closed off. Kali didn't know what was going through Mary's mind.

The trauma and horror of this experience ripped Kali's life inside out. Usually a strong, healthy woman accustomed to a lot of mountain biking, climbing, and skiing, Kali developed food sensitivities and allergic reactions to countless things, as well as severe adrenal fatigue that plagued her long afterward. She found basic decisions difficult, and her therapeutic massage job overwhelming. Within six months of Mary's death, Kali had to stop working and move back home for almost a year.

Kali remembers, "My body was literally shutting down from the trauma, grief, and illness that followed. At one point, [my doctor] considered hospitalization. [At the time of this writing,] I still cannot work more than four days a week due to the fatigue it places on my body. I never believed in post-traumatic stress disorder until this. Although I was diagnosed with it, I didn't completely accept it till I began to experience the triggers that would send me spinning for days, weeks, and even months."

If she could talk to Mary today, Kali says she would tell her, "In a way, you not only take your own life but also steal from the lives of the people who loved you so deeply. Now they not only have to deal with living but surviving after a part of them has been stripped away, never to return. Suicide may seem to take away your pain - I can only hope that it does - but know this: You leave even more pain behind."

If you feel alone, like your life doesn't matter and you are better off dead because you believe no one cares about you, stop.

Right now. Please stop.

Please do not follow through with your suicide attempt! Have you told anyone how hopeless you feel?

If you haven't, you owe it to yourself and those who love you to at least open up and reach out for help. People around you may not be aware of your hopelessness. Please tell them!

Give your friends a chance to help you. I would give anything to have had that chance with Katrina. A woman seriously considering suicide said, "I picked up my phone and talked to a friend about I feel.. And in the process [I] realized I am not alone in this situation. I never knew just talking to someone would be a world of difference."

You are not alone. You are precious and your life is invaluable. Someone loves you, more than you know!

And there is hope! People who have a suicide plan and wait on it generally find purpose to keep living. Most of your problems are temporary, even though they don't seem like it in the moment. They *will* eventually be resolved. I have seen this so many times in my own life. Is it really worth giving up your precious life to get away from these problems?

If you die, what will you face? You've escaped from your problems on earth, but now what?

If there's an afterlife, then what happens? If there's a God - you can't conclusively prove there isn't - you must face him. Your life is not your own! It belongs to God. He chose to breathe you into existence, and He is the reason your heart beats life throughout your body day in and day out. He created you for a good purpose, far greater than despair and suicide. He says, "For I know the plans I have for you...plans to prosper you and not to harm you, plans to give you hope and a future" (Jer. 29:11).

I can't say with complete certainty that Katrina is in heaven. I don't know her final thoughts. When it was too late, did she regret what she'd done and silently ask God's forgiveness? How did He receive her? What did He say?

In C.S. Lewis's novel, *The Horse and His Boy*, an orphan, Shasta, has been separated from his friend, Aravis, after a frightening night journey through the desert. Shasta doesn't know where Aravis is or if she is all right. He asks Aslan (the God-character of the novel) what will happen to her.

Aslan answers, "Child, I am telling you your story, not hers. No one is told any story but their own."

We don't get to see every outcome of other people's choices or the deepest motives of their hearts. We can only look from the outside and guess at whether they know and want God.

I believe Katrina faced God's perfect justice mixed with mercy. I know enough about God to trust that He will decide what is wisest and most loving to do for my sister in the afterlife. I know that

122

she will stand in His presence, be humbled by His holiness, and answer for what she has done. Not just for her death, but for every choice she made before that.

So will I, someday. So will you.

"Today, if you hear His voice, do not harden your hearts." (Heb. 3:15) Be reconciled to God! He is the source of every goodness and hope. He loves you with a passion deeper and bigger than you can imagine. "For if, while we were God's enemies, we were reconciled to him through the death of his Son, how much more, having been reconciled, shall we be saved through his life!" (Romans 5:10)

Attempting suicide does not set anything right - with God or with troubles on earth. It can be a permanent mistake made trying to fix temporary problems.

Please choose life with me!

Ten

Brown-Sugar Blessings
My journey of grief and joy – the first five months

I would have despaired unless I had believed that I would see the goodness of the Lord in the land of the living. Psalm 27:13

While in college, Katrina wrote to a friend,

That reminds me of something I heard recently... A speaker here said, "If you put a bowl of white sugar and a bowl of brown sugar in front of someone who had never seen sugar before, and you told this person to choose one of them, which one would he pick? Probably the white sugar because it sparkles, it looks pure, and it's attractive. The brown sugar looks like dirt. But the brown sugar has a wonderful flavor, which is why we like using it when we bake.

"The white sugar represents the obvious blessings in our lives. But there are also hard times, when we cry out in pain to God, asking, 'Why, God? I don't understand.' Often it's years later – sometimes five, ten years, or even right on our deathbed – that we see the results of those hardships and realize that they were actually blessings. They were brown-sugar blessings... important to the overall flavor of the cookie. God wants us to taste just right when we come out of the oven."

Here is my book of grief, recording the brown-sugar blessings that came out of Katrina's death. As I open its pages for you to read, please look through these words written by me at age seventeen, and see that I was fumbling to understand that I'd just been trapped into a different life because of my sister's choice. Even today I sometimes get tired of being the woman whose sister committed suicide, and I wish I could shake off the burden that has come with it. Selfishly, I wish I could skip the public speaking about Katrina, which I fear, and having to push myself to write this book, which was painful.

But for reasons I will never know, God stood there while Katrina breathed in helium and breathed out life, and didn't interfere with her choice to die. He let her go.

125

He has helped me live. And that is why I need you to meet me here near the end of the book, because I want you to choose life with me. It is not going to be the pain free life you hope for, but I promise Father God will be there, offering Himself, His very person of love, as a guide and comfort through whatever pain comes.

Nov. 17, 2001
Dear Katrina,

Tonight Rebecca and I are sleeping in your and Rachel's room. We sure made a mess moving things around…you didn't leave much behind, Katrina. I wish you'd left a letter for me instead of your wardrobe, an explanation rather than your textbooks and the potholders you crocheted.

O Katrina, did you really truly understand the depth of our love for you that Friday evening? If you had, you wouldn't have gone. Now I must wait, maybe many years, to see you again and to say, "I love you." Yours is the joy, mine is the sacrifice and the ache. Is it a fair exchange? I don't know. It's a risky thing to call anything fair in this world of evil and injustice.

Anyway, about our new sleeping arrangements…when we got home last night from Indiana, we were ready for some changes. Rachel didn't like sleeping in her old room alone, especially with all her memories of you to keep her lonely. So Rebecca and I decided to move permanently. Now our bunk bed sits in one corner and Rachel's bed in another.

Katrina, is it really true that I can't ever hug you again? You won't be getting off the plane in December to greet us with your beautiful smile?

I ache. Mama is crying again. Sometimes I want to say you were cruel to go so soon and give us this daily heartache. But I can't. You weren't cruel, only irrational, helpless, confused, and guilty. What were you guilty of? Unforgivable sins? No. But that must have been how you saw them. *Grace* was a vague term to you.

Goodnight. I want to come to you soon.

Nov. 19

Today it is a month since you died. I believe with all my feeble human faith that you are in heaven – but I still find it all so surreal.

Katrina, are you dead? Did you really leave me?

I cannot imagine the pain of those who lost dear ones in the

World Trade Center. The coroner from Muncie, Indiana, who came to the scene when you were found, said that those people in New York still can't accept the reality of their loved one's death...there was no body to see, no shred of evidence to convince those yet living that a certain person had actually died. Theirs is the nightmare of "whys" and agonizing nights and hopeless hope.

I saw you. I don't remember your face – I'm glad I don't – but I remember your stiffly unnatural body. Your skin was its usual cold mottled color, and your chest was raised, as if you died partway through a breath. I recall how your hands were folded across your stomach – oh, Katrina, they should have been an old woman's hands, not sensitive, agile, young hands. You still had a faint pale line on your wrist, marking where your watch used to be. Do you remember how we used to compare our wristwatch tan marks to see who had the greater contrast between brown and white?

You wore your pink graduation dress. It didn't complement your figure as it had in your grad picture. Everything about you *wasn't* you. And I'm glad for that. I want to remember you as you were in life, not in death.

At the graveside service, I rejoiced that I didn't have to say goodbye to you before you were lowered into your allotted piece of ground. "From dust to dust returneth," they say. So many people say their final goodbye at the burial because they have no confidence of eternity. For them, the soul is buried with the body. And they who remain have to release an entire person, body and soul. But you were given over to Jesus fifteen years ago. We had no doubts as we drove away from the cemetery.

See you later, Katrina.

Nov. 20

We were only leaving your body behind, after all. Your soul was with Jesus.

You know how focused and persevering you were when it came to school? Well, I find it difficult to be either today, when you are so much on my mind. I can't concentrate on any one thing for more than fifteen minutes. I flutter from one task to the next.

Last night Rachel, Rebecca and I were goofing off and teasing each other (sound familiar?), and I piped up once with the memory of you calling me your "pet peeve." You and I got along so well, Katrina. I'm just sorry that I'm the one who has to store away all our memories of doing things together – that we can't make any

127

more memories. We were going to grow old and become crotchety old maids and share a house, remember? Even as we joked about it, I knew it wouldn't come true. With your inner and outer beauty, I knew some special man would find you sooner or later and put an end to our crotchety spinster scheme.

Nov. 21

It's our cousin Jerod's eighteenth birthday today. I remember how he and his sister Jenny came to the house that Saturday morning when we had just found out about you. They were so good to us, just being there. I knew it was hard for them, too, not knowing exactly what to say. Jenny was still trying to fathom the fact that she had just lost her best childhood friend. She regretted that you never got to hold her baby.

Daddy and Mama needed our help that day. I haven't seen them so helpless before, but I thank God that He gave us enough strength so Daddy and Mama could lean on us. Rebecca and I were the "rememberers" when other memories failed. We did the little things, cleaned up the house to get ready for whoever might come in the next week, suggested people to call, etc. I don't know how we did it. My only explanation is that "we have this treasure in jars of clay to show that this all-surpassing power is from God and not from us." (2 Cor. 4:7) It wasn't *us* doing these things.

Because at that point, all I wanted to do was go hole myself up somewhere and die. If you weren't alive, there seemed no point in my living any longer either.

Yet, in this intense trial, I really began to experience what Phil. 4:7 talks about: "And the peace of God, which transcends all understanding, will guard your hearts and your minds in Christ Jesus."

Nov. 22

Remember how I used to call you "Josephine"? I don't know how I got away with it when you were so strict about being plain Jane "Katrina." You wouldn't even answer Rebecca if she slurred over your name and it came out as a lazy "Gu-treena." Anyway. I called you "Josephine" because you and the name suited each other somehow. I suppose you both created the image of a true lady. So, I wrote this poem to you. There is a relief in saying some things in poems.

128

Josephine

You were a lady at a proper masquerade,
We thought the mask before us was truly your own face.
But you deceived us—and you never laid
aside the shimmering, feathery illusion.

We danced till the wee hours of dawn,
which to you was the blackest of nights.
Then, silently, you waltzed out to the lawn
And began your last dance...all alone.

No one missed your presence at first.
Unaware, we continued our frolicking.
Then an uninvited guest arrived, and he burst
our bubble of merriment with his news.

The music came to an abrupt halt—
one violin bow gave a last scrape across the strings—
The stranger begged our pardon: it was entirely his fault
for interrupting our gaiety and dancing.

He started to tell his news and as we listened,
one by one we removed our gaudy masks.
Behind the stiff grinning faces, tears glistened
on real cheeks, and weeping began where laughter had been.

Our joyous morning turned into your weary night
when the stranger had finished his story.
The brilliant sunrise came, and the light
glittered through the windows. But we did not see.

Miss Josephine, you went and we stayed.
Why didn't you invite us along?
Heartbroken in the midst of our masquerade,
The elaborate ballroom no longer suited our mood.

Standing among the remnants of party things,
we heard again—over and over and over—
that violin bow's last scrape across the strings.

It mournfully echoed, and we blamed ourselves.

Your little hints of departure were coming back
in full force to our minds. And we blamed
ourselves, for we had treated you with such a lack
of understanding. *We should have known.*

You were the mysterious lady at the ball,
Miss Josephine, whom no one really knew.
Behind your mask was a sad face, but you refused to call
for someone to help remove the stiff, grinning illusion.

And so you left us, and we stay…surrounded by
Mocking reminders of a happier day.
In our shimmering costumes, we all cry—
Since the night that Miss Josephine died.

   I wrote the following poem after finishing "Josephine."
Mama had just showed me a small pocketknife found among your
things. The knife had dark stains along the blade. Was it blood?
Mama held it out to me, but I didn't want to look closer. In your last
letter to us, you said you'd tried to slit your wrists before finding a
better way to end your life. If this pocketknife was what you used, I
wanted it far, far away from me. Saying nothing about the nausea I
felt, I quickly ended the conversation with Mama, and she took the
hated thing away. She didn't mean to hurt me – for some reason, she
was ready to see that knife and I wasn't. I'd say that grief is "funny"
the way it works, but right now, it's just plain horrible.

I'm not ready…

so don't push me into what I cannot handle.
the bile rises in my throat—I choke.
I can't breathe, inside or out. Don't
force on me the ugly things now; it is hard
enough to bear the facts already given.
My mind refuses to receive the reality
That an object of attempted suicide presents.
In front of my eyes?—no, no, <u>no</u>!
Do not put it there! I don't want to see it yet.
I never want to see it.

But I just did.
I cringe inside, patching vainly the
hole in my self-protection bubble. It is
enough for me to have head knowledge; I need
nothing else at this point.
Please.... try to understand where I am
coming from. This is too much for me, although
it may be what you need to heal. All it does
to me is widen the hole of grief in my heart, stretch
out my pain. I hurt and cry.

Nov. 24

Katrina, because you left, I am becoming a new person. I wrote the following prayer in my journal, "...for out of these ashes You alone can bring beauty." Isaiah 61:3 says, "To bestow on them a crown of beauty instead of ashes..." I praise the Savior for all He has revealed to me about Himself since you died! Of course, there is also the wish that you did not have to die for these changes to come about. But again, I know God doesn't always direct the courses of our lives according to our wishes. You wished for an easy out, and you found one.

I wrote earlier about how those who have no hope grieve, and how they must say goodbye to the departed. Because of Christ, I am not one of those people; I will *not* wear a crown of ashes, an attitude of deep mourning and despair before God. I *will* wear instead a crown of *beauty*! It is a reality that I see happening in my life right now, but I still find it all incomprehensible.

I went for a walk this morning down the snow-frosted road, and I poured my heart out to the One who always listens. I didn't try to hide anything... all my confusion, how I felt that I no longer had an identity because the person by whom I knew myself was gone, all my feelings about your absence, my changed responses to the world around me.

I gave everything to Him. Then I stood still and listened to the peaceful hillsides around me, to the honk of a passing goose overhead. Even the dusting of snow was eloquent. I began to sing, "Praise to the Lord, the Almighty, the King of creation." But for the first time, I was so overwhelmed by the sense of the One I was singing to that I just started crying. "Why do You love me?" For the first time, I found it incomprehensible that Jesus Christ died for me and that He is truly the High Priest who understands, because He entered our world of hurt.

Nov. 25

We went to church today and couldn't concentrate on much of anything, least of all the sermon. Daddy closed his eyes and rested, while Rachel managed to take notes and listen. I listened but got distracted by the littlest things. Mama stayed home because she was so tired, and she didn't think she could handle the stress of driving to town on the snowy roads.

Snow covers a bleak landscape and magically turns it into a soft, white world. In a way, that is like our lives after you died. Without Jesus, we would have had only bleak landscapes to look at. But through His boundless, unfathomable grace, tragedy is softened and we are faced with an incredibly beautiful world to continue living in.

True, we have to wade through the drifts to get to our goal, and sometimes I know we'll flounder about aimlessly. But He put those drifts in our path, so He will carry us through. This is similar to, but not as good as your "brown sugar blessings" example that you heard at college.

Nov. 27

These days I find it incredible that a person is actually capable of concentrating on a task at hand for a long time. Now as I try, over and over, to do my school, I am amazed at how David found stamina to go back into college life. Ten days after your death, he was going to classes again. No wonder he had such a struggle to make the transition!

When he comes home, Lord willing, on the 13th we will probably head over to Bible camp for a week. None of us feel in a very "Christmassy" mood and it will be hard to have this first Christmas at home without you. We thought that getting away would be good. I think what I will enjoy most is the solitude; I've allowed myself to go without it and also without time for God...which is what I need most. Like Paul (but in a different context), I do what I do not want to do, but what I want to do, I do not do. (Rom. 7:15)

I love you dearly, Katrina. The numbness is there again, so I don't feel your absence as on other days. Have I even had enough time to think about it?

Nov. 29

The sun is setting earlier every day, so it's always around dusk that I get outside for a walk and some fresh air. Last night I half-wanted to go sledding a couple of times on Daisy's Hill. But the desire was quickly quenched when I thought of you and how, when we were little, we used to sled all afternoon until it became dark outside and our snow clothes were wet from playing in the snow. Will there be some things that I'll never go back to because I'm afraid? Or because I'm ready to move on to different things?

I want to cry. But when I most want to pour out my heart in tears, I can't. And when I don't want to cry, I always end up getting teary-eyed anyway.

"O God, please, *please* let me cry!" Let me feel *pain*. Please.

I'm afraid that if I go back to my normal bedtime routine, another police officer will come and start the nightmare all over again. There's nothing I can do to prevent the Almighty from carrying out His purposes, but sometimes I want to believe that such a thing is possible.

Memories will come and go; it hurts to even acknowledge the fact that I won't remember everything about you, no matter how close we were. But I will always have one memory, for as long as I live... of the morning we were told that you died.

Ron and Jean sat there, listening but not saying a word. I wanted to scream out, "What's wrong with you? Why did you come here if you won't hold us, if you won't cry with us? Are you devoid of feelings?" For me, the pain and reality was fresh, throbbing. Ron and Jean had heard the news several hours ago and were now in shock over it. They were probably unable to comfort us.

Minutes after the officer had said you were dead, I knew exactly what I needed to tell him. I knew, without a doubt, that you would have wanted me to ask. And if I failed to do so, I would have failed and disappointed you, who always had more faith in me than I really deserved.

Then, incredibly, I was given the opportunity. Jeff stood up and said, "Are there any other questions you have for me?"

I choked out, "If you died tonight, where would you go?" My words frightened me – was I really asking this question? How could I ask it *now*? He couldn't understand me at first and had me repeat what I said; I found it so hard to speak.

He replied, "Well, I hope I'd go to heaven."

"How do you know?"

"Because I have faith in God."

133

I forget what he said after that – something about *strong* faith in God, and then I finished by saying, "I just wanted to make sure that *you* know for sure."

He was puzzled, I could tell, but very gracious and considerate to a girl who was clearly not thinking straight. Well, dear Katrina, I was a fool for Christ the morning after you went to be with our Savior. And I want to keep on being His fool, but sometimes I find it hard not to conform and be "normal" like everyone else.

"For since, in the wisdom of God, the world through wisdom did not know God, it pleased God through the foolishness of the message preached to save those who believed…Because the foolishness of God is wiser than men, and the weakness of God is stronger than men." (1 Cor. 1:21, 25)

Dec. 4

Mama asked me yesterday what I missed most about you. I had to think for a long time to choose only a few things. I miss *everything* about you, good and bad. But I said that I missed your quiet rebukes to Rebecca and me when we were teasing and pestering each other: Like little kids, we were reminded to "grow up!" I also miss how you balanced me: where you were strong, I was weak and vice versa. A while ago, I made one of my startling comments – said that I wondered whether I'd marry someone almost like you – who had your temperament and personality. But – one exception. My desire is that Mr. Right will have a deeper maturity in Christ than either you or I do. I want to be led. I don't want to lead. I want to look forward and follow, not look behind to see if I'm being faithfully followed.

Aunt Debbie observed that when Rachel, Rebecca, and I are old and getting gray, you'll still be nineteen. Photos of you will only ever show a young girl. This is an obvious fact, but I had to say it, so I could grasp the reality of it. You knew so well what pictures meant to me. And now I won't see any more new ones of you.

Dec. 6

"The Lord brings death and makes alive; He brings down to the grave and raises up." (1 Sam. 2:6)

Yesterday I wrote a little "essay" about you. Words make me cry when sights and sounds can't reach me.

Can I ask you something? I want to know if it is selfish for me to write about myself so often… Under the present circumstances

134

I have a magnified fear of treading on others' sensitive feelings. Relationships can be the gnarliest, most tangled-up skeins you could ever involve yourself in. (Take it from someone on her way to becoming an expert about it.) And now little things I never thought much about before (such as writing or talking about myself) are suddenly of utmost importance. Every little word that comes out of this mouth demands to be thought over first. People are such touchy creatures; life itself is a headache. "Blessed are the hermits, for theirs is true peace."

A natural way to react to pain and harsh words from others is to lash out – or cower in a corner. I want to lash out so badly – to scream out the pain inside, blame everyone for hurting me with their hurts. *Cushion me, please. Make my life easy.*

What I am struggling through now is completely different from your own struggles. But I can now know what you felt. No wonder you escaped it all. I understand, even while I continue to believe that your choice of escape was wrong. My escape may be this: To walk through the hardships and come out on the other side. In a way, it is an escape – it's an escape from my old man, my sinful nature… but it's still a hard, hard way to go.

Dec. 10

I'm trying to study physics…not working.

Do you know what I regret most right now about you being gone? I regret not having talked to you on the phone more faithfully or written you emails more often. Not that it necessarily would have made a whole lot of difference in the outcome – but you deserved these things. As my sister, especially.

I struggle to open up and express my love more. For me it's like laying my soul naked for all the curious onlookers to study. I feel foolish for not being able to readily share with my family how much they mean to me. It's like cracking a nut that's reluctant to open because it is so accustomed to being sealed shut. "Lord, make me open. I find it hard to do it myself."

I am so tired today. Tired of the same pain of loss day after day; tired of hoping certain people will reach out and comfort us and then feeling guilty and ungrateful when others do the comforting; tired of expecting more from people and being disappointed; tired of bearing many burdens; tired of each "blah" day that melds into the next; tired of feeling lazy and helpless; tired of living a different "normal" from the world's "normal"; tired of thinking about me;

tired of being angry; tired of being tired.

"Come unto Me, all you who are weary and heavy-laden, and I will give you rest. For My burden is light, and My yoke is easy." (Matt. 11:28)

And somewhere, in my tiredness, I feel a responsibility to always have you on my mind and to be pushing out thoughts of myself to make room for thoughts of others. Where is the line of balance?

Being able to pour all of these thoughts and feelings out is a big release for me. They've been a leaden weight in my mind, a constant burden that I carry around wherever I go. As I've said before, writing is my vent for most things. Once I've got something down on paper, part of the load on my heart is gone. I thank God for giving me this outlet. If I'd never discovered it, I think I would have exploded a long time ago from a build-up of internal emotions.

Much as I'm crunched for time, I still feel the need to write out in detail what I've experienced and learned. It bothers me that I can't be as chronological or clear as I'd like, but you'll just have to bear with me. My mind isn't all here, yet. That's how it's been for all of us—our mind has a short in its thought circuit, but our mouth keeps talking or our pen keeps writing, and we never notice the mistake we just made. I'm learning to live with it and not knock myself over the head when it happens, because I know I can't help it.

"God, help me to run to You and hide in You, because You are stable, constant."

Dec. 11

Our parting reminds me of the parting between Frodo and Sam in *The Return of the King*. Frodo chose to leave Middle Earth because he was searching for rest from his wounds and burdens. And Sam, faithful, loving companion, was to stay behind because his place was still in Middle Earth. I remember we read Tolkien's trilogy when we were younger, and it took *forever* and got to be *so* boring. Now that I'm older, I appreciate it more. Tolkien had the ability to create a new world with characters we could relate to perfectly.

But, again back to Frodo and Sam. They said farewell to each other at the Grey Havens and Sam stood on the shore, watching Frodo sail away to the mysterious land of eternal rest. I never got to say goodbye as you left this world. Perhaps it was better that way. The hurt now might only have been greater if I had been with you, though I think that the end result would have been entirely different:

136

I couldn't have sat there and just let you go.

Dec. 17

Aside from all the blundering thoughts, I still think of you and miss you. We decorated Christmas cookies on Saturday, but it was very different from last year. We didn't talk a whole lot or joke around. Mama took pictures and we smiled cheerily, but behind the smile, I could only think of the person who was missing from our fun. And I ached.

I never thought that the gradual healing would hurt so much, either. "How could I go on with life and not have Katrina on my mind all the time?" I ask myself. I'm no longer consumed with thoughts of you, and though I know the healing is a healthy thing, it still hurts to realize that life will go on but you won't. Eventually, you will fade from some people's memories or be forgotten altogether. We won't ever forget you, but others will. I guess it just seems callous to push ahead and leave you behind. But I have to, in some ways. I can't go on living in the past.

We had a family meeting last night, and Rebecca was acting hilariously goofy. I wish you had been there to laugh with us and add to our silliness. Your laugh was so unique, but I can't remember it right now. I do remember how your eye (right or left?) would close when you were laughing especially hard. We teased you about it and you got tired of the teasing, so we stopped.

How I want a hearty cry! Just to sob out everything inside would be a blessed release. At least then I'd know I had some sensitivity, some feelings left. I want to visit you, too. I'm mean, what's left of you here. I'm glad you're happy. Today I'm not.

Brine

Tears bring
release from pain, don't they?
But they sting…
with the brine of an
Ocean of sorrow in my eyes.

Dec. 26

I am having a very lovely pity party down here in the guestroom reading *The Return of the King*, sipping chicken broth and trying to ignore my nasty old cold. After I finish this entry I'll be going to rest my weary bones; they feel leaden tonight.

But first I want to write down something Frodo said to Sam after Sam learned that his master was going to the Havens and wouldn't be taking him along, "Your time may come. Do not be too sad, Sam. You cannot be always torn in two. You will have to be one and whole, for many years. You have so much to enjoy, and to be, and to do." When Sam replied that he thought Frodo would live to a ripe old age in the Shire, Frodo answers, "So I thought, too, once. But I have been too deeply hurt, Sam." In my heart, I know that I am to stay behind while you live beyond the Havens.

When we were over at camp, I missed your presence often while we did things as a family. Knowing that one person was gone sometimes took the enthusiasm away and left only a humdrum activity to do. I wish you had been there to play hockey, despite the fact that you'd have been a most proper and gentle player.

We listened to an audio drama of *Les Misérables* on tape yesterday; I cried at the end when Valjean died, honored and loved too late, a misunderstood and rejected man. Sort of like you. You died a rather lonely death. At least Valjean had the one most precious to him by his side as he left the world. You had only a car ceiling to look at…Oh, it is morbid to think of that.

Dec. 31

"He is carried to the grave, and watch is kept over his tomb. The soil in the valley is sweet to him; all men follow after him, and a countless throng goes before him." (Job 21:32, 33)

Yesterday we were driving out to Grandpa and Grandma's place when Mama asked David and me if we wanted to visit your grave. David responded, "It really doesn't matter if I go or not. She isn't there." Just like that – plain as plain. At first I didn't really know what to say. Then I decided not to say anything, because he and I have different feelings about it. I agree with him that you're not there. But I also, for one time at least, want to be one who keeps watch over your tomb. And maybe when I visit the cemetery (I haven't been to your grave since the burial service), I'll decide that I don't really need to come either…that the places and times I will remember and mourn you will be anywhere but beside your grave. I don't know. But I *will* come one day.

Tomorrow begins a new year: Rachel will be working at the restaurant in Cut Bank till midnight; Daddy and David are also in town taking care of farm business; Rebecca and Mama are doing a math lesson in the schoolroom. Tomorrow we will each be doing something else, but we'll all be reminded that a new year has begun and you are not there to be part of it.

You would have been a college junior in the fall of 2003. You'd have taken more art classes and the year following you'd have had your own senior art display in the main hall of the art building. Now I realize how much I looked forward to seeing you become a better artist and be recognized for your talent; I'm sorry that will never happen. And as for music, I already knew that you were very gifted at the piano. I remember the first time you played your piano composition, *Melody*, for us when you came home for Christmas last year. I was awed: Did *my* sister really write that? Wow. No other piano pieces will follow *Melody*, as I'd hoped.

Jan. 2

I remember the turnover from an old year to a new used to be an exciting thing for me. It gave me the chance to read back through my journal, seeing how I'd grown and in what areas I still needed to grow. Then I'd carefully write out my New Year's resolutions, which were always more like mental reminders than anything else. I haven't been able to write the resolutions yet because I'm still catching up in my journal from our Indiana trip – the last such trip I hope we'll ever take.

I say "used to" and "was" quite often now as I look back on things I did before you died. Nearly all of them have changed for me. The new year holds no excitement, only dull apathy. My spirit rises joyfully less often; I don't have as many gleeful moments like I once did. I hope God will bring some of that back to me... I miss my old self – carefree, lively, spontaneous. Of course, I don't want all of it to be the same as it was before you died. Some of me died when you did, and maybe that's a good thing. I think God is purging out the dross.

Last night Mama and I talked for a while about you. I mentioned wanting to have lunch in town with her sometime and she suggested we do it on my birthday.

When she said, "your eighteenth birthday," I began to cry. I hurt so deeply, realizing that you would never turn twenty and that in two years I will be older than you. I *hate* it! I hate it that nothing in my future will be part of your life. I hate it that I will live longer than you, know more than you did, experience more than you were able to, and never sit beside you at the dining room table again. That is what I enjoyed so much when you were home – just being near you, as if to say to the rest of the world, "This is my sister – Katrina!"

And I *hate* past tenses, too.

Jan. 3

Here is something I wrote about Mama yesterday: "Hers, to all appearances, was true sorrow. No one could be confused by her tears or spoken memories and pains. They were very clear. As for the rest of us – well, we were each a rare case. Our separate grief diagnoses would have befuddled both our doctor and us. I wish I could grieve like my mother and have a 'normal,' predictable grief. Mine, however, can't be moved from its natural course without damage to me. So I have to go on, and sorrow alone because my pain is too unique to be shared."

Anyway, it's just a little thing I wrote – for all that it's worth.

I'd like to write down some of the verses and passages that have lifted me up after you died. Some of them practically leapt off the pages as I read through the Psalms. Rebecca and I sat down in the schoolroom the morning we heard about you and read and read and read out of the Psalms. We couldn't get enough of them. I could truly *feel* my heart being comforted and rested.

"You, O Lord, keep my lamp burning; my God turns my darkness into light...as for God, His way is perfect." (Ps. 18:28, 30)

"Keep me as the apple of your eye; hide me in the shadow of your wings." (Ps. 17:8)

"And with it you shall make incense, a perfume, the work of a perfumer, salted – pure – and holy. And you shall beat some of it very fine..." (Ex. 30:35, 36) A reminder of our Christian witness (salt) and how God refines us to make us more holy and better witnesses.

"To the Lord I cry aloud, and He answers me from His holy hill." (Ps. 3:4)

"They that sow in tears shall reap in joy." (Ps. 126:5)

"Many are asking, 'Who can show us any good?' Let the light of your face shine upon us..." (Ps. 4:6)

Jan. 10

We are on our way home from the city and there is the sun setting in the west, an amber lozenge resting in blue-gray clouds above the mountains. And up there – somewhere outside our sky and

140

beyond our sunsets you are with your Savior.

Sometimes I think of you as I last saw you, the breath of life gone, leaving you cold and unnatural-looking. If I let myself, I think I could remember what you looked like. But I never dare to dwell on the thought long enough to allow the image of you into my mind. Other times, at odd moments, I wish you were there to talk to; I find something that you'd enjoy hearing about, but then with a pang, your absence hits me.

Do you know we can't ever talk again until I come to you?

Jan. 17

I felt like a hypocrite after writing the above, because there seemed to be no emotion inside me; I did not truly miss you at that moment. And I try to never write what is not reality.

Today I long for you. The longing has eaten at my thoughts, my everyday activities so that I couldn't ignore it. I miss you. For the rest of my life, everything will be measured by your absence. Sometimes I will feel it less and be distracted by what's going on around me. The voices of others will drown out my thoughts of you just as they will occasionally bring to mind reminders of you and make me cry.

I will never forget that one moment yesterday, when I saw life as it was before you died. I woke up from a nap and for one wonderful instant I believed nothing had ever happened. Just a dream, right? The pain of waking to reality was piercing. It's tempting to pretend nothing ever happened, to enter a dream world where you still exist.

But that's like running to the elusive sunset. I'll never totally escape the reality of you being gone.

"God, all I want today is to talk to my Katrina. That's all. I never got to say goodbye. You were separated from Christ for three days before He conquered sin and rose from the grave, but I am separated from Katrina for a lifetime. O Jesus, please come soon! Or help me bear this loneliness and longing."

Sometimes I feel like I left the world of life and now dwell in the land of the shadow of death, where light and dark are unveiled.

On December 4th, I was writing about you and me and Mr. Right. In reading the entry again, I remembered the odd wish I've had at the back of my mind for a while: I wish I could meet the man God intended for you to marry. All I want is to meet him. Is it a foolish desire?

What I said about you living beyond the sunset and clouds made me think of when Grandma Hamm died. I was eight at the time, I think. For a long time after her funeral, I would pause and look up at the sky when it was overcast and search for a little opening in the clouds. If I found one, I was elated, thinking, "Grandma has her very own window to look through so she can watch us." And I wondered if she could see me looking up from the earth. Those childish imaginings were a comfort to me, for at that time, Grandma was the only person of real importance to me who had died. And I am still comforted by seeing a "window" in the clouds; it reminds me of your happiness, though I've left behind the belief that you can peep through and see me.

Jan. 24

Even these orderly entries are becoming disorganized...I can't seem to hold it all together these days.

Tonight I was listening to the last audio drama tape of Dietrich Bonhoeffer's life and heard the following: "They shall grow not old as we that are left grow old. Age shall not weary them, nor the years condemn. At the going down of the sun and in the morning – we shall remember them." As usual, I cried.

Feb. 1

I'm sitting by your grave as I write this. It is cold, and getting colder as the sun sinks behind the clouds. I won't be able to stay as long as I wanted to.

Well, I'm as close to you right now as I'll ever be for the rest of my life. I guess the reason I never came to the cemetery till now is that I want to think of *you* – not your body – as you are. When I am here, in the sanctuary of the dead, that is how I think of you: dead. But you're ALIVE! More alive than I, half-frozen already, am this very minute. It's strange how things change. I used to walk across cemeteries without a thought for the dead bodies half a fathom beneath my feet. Now I feel guilty for stepping over graves, as if I'm desecrating something sacred.

Feb. 12

If healing has anything to do with writing less often, then I must be healing. God has been SO good to me the past two or three weeks. He's given me joy, a renewed interest in school and other projects, the ability to look forward, as well as backward. If healing

142

means leaving the cemetery with a lighter heart, then God must be healing me.

Yet I envy you; I wish I could be with you. Heaven holds no sorrow, but every street down here is full of unhappy people. I am glad God can use me to help others find joy...When you died, we were admitted to a world where girls struggle with eating disorders and feel the same things you felt. We are always discovering another person who needs help. The wonderful thing is that we know how to help, at least a little bit.

Feb. 19

Last night I dreamed that our family visited the old ghost town of Bannack again. You know, that place in southern Montana we stopped at on our way home from California last spring? Anyway, I dreamed that you and I were trying to find the building where Mama had taken a picture of us. We wanted to have another picture taken at the same spot, but it took us such a long time to find it. We never got our second picture. I knew you weren't really there with us, even in the dream. But the feeling of looking, looking, looking for that particular old building made me feel as if I were actually looking for you.

I woke up dissatisfied and unhappy.

A few weeks after that visit to Bannack (the real life visit, I mean), you finished high school, and the four of us girls sang "The Blessing of the Lord" at your commencement. This May, David is graduating from LeTourneau University and we're all going down to Texas for that. A few weeks afterward, I will graduate in Kalispell. Maybe we can, if we are able to handle it, sing "The Blessing of the Lord" again. You are so much a part of my life that when I think of me, you come to mind, and when I tell others how I'm doing, I usually mention you and how much I miss you.

" 'I miss you.' O God, words are so hollow, especially those three." They can never adequately describe what it feels like to hear Daddy weeping at night or to cry until I must gasp for breath, or to lie beside Rebecca on her bed, but unable to carry my sister's sorrow because my own is enough to handle right then.

Your friend Amanda called yesterday; she and I visited for quite a while and I was so glad to hear her voice again. She told me that David had recently sent her a thank you note for the birthday gift she gave him. When she read the card, she cried for a long time because David's handwriting looked so much like yours. She also misses you and hurts at your loss.

Feb. 20

"The Lord gave and the Lord has taken away; may the name of the Lord be praised." (Job 1:21)

Today would have been your golden birthday. I cried this afternoon, but didn't try to find the reason for my tears....sometimes there is no reason.

Joyful gratitude mingles with weary sadness in my soul. The gratitude comes from an outpouring of love from people who know that today you would have turned twenty. They put aside their own cares for a moment just to give us a call, write us a note, pray for our comfort: It is such a precious thing to know that others are grieving with us. The love comes from people I never imagined would reach out with such warm compassion.

Just after lunch, our cousin Chantry came over and handed me a card, adding that he and his wife Kara were praying for us today. I know he felt a little awkward in not knowing what to say, but the fact that he cared and is grieving, too – that is immeasurably precious. I went back to the piano after he left and began to cry as I played "For All the Saints."

Chantry's gesture made me think how unworthy we, especially, are to receive so much love. But on a grander scale, it makes me think of how mankind doesn't deserve God's grace, yet He gives it freely. None of us deserve His love, which was demonstrated to us by the cross.

What of the weary sadness, then, if I am a child of the promise and have my name written on the palms of the Almighty? The world makes me sad by the burden of sin it carries and refuses to give up. There is nothing uplifting about watching the havoc wreaked by evil. I'm weary of this world where I am a stranger, and I long for Home. Yet God still calls me to service, to draw more into His kingdom...I feel – no, I *am* – so unworthy to serve Him. "Oh, Jesus, I long to be perfectly whole."

"I would have lost heart unless I had believed that I would see the goodness of the Lord in the land of the living." (Ps. 27:13)

"Oh, how great is your goodness, which you have laid up for those who fear you, which you have prepared for those who trust in you in the presence of the sons of men!" (Ps. 31:19)

The following poem describes so well the weariness I

144

feel…as if I am trapped in a self-built cage with the equal desires of getting out and staying in. Every day is a carbon copy of the last one. Little stones of blessing can't seem to cause ripples in the smooth surface of monotonous life. I am tired of living and want to go Home.

From *Later Life*
Something in this foggy day, a something which
  Is neither of this fog nor of today…
I am sick of where I am and where I am not
  I am sick of foresight and of memory,
  I am sick of all I have and all I see,
    I am sick of self, and there is nothing new;
Oh weary impatient patience of my lot!—
    Thus with myself: how fares it, Friends, with you?

Christina G. Rossetti

So you would have been twenty down here on earth…so what? Does that matter anything to you? The other day I read John's description of heaven, and, like many other things have, the passage took on a new meaning. *You* are walking those streets of gold, *you* are eating the fruit of the trees, *and you* are seeing the gates made of single pearls and the walls of lovely stone. *You are in His presence.* What birthday gift could be greater than that?

Feb. 27
Now, near the end of this letter to you, I am experiencing "joy unspeakable" along with the sorrow. Sometimes the two are so intertwined I can't separate them. Reminds me of the quote, "The deeper sorrow carves into your being, the more joy you can contain."

This morning before my alarm clock went off, I had the most amazing dream…another answer to prayer. In my dream I was with friends from Big Sky Bible Institute, but *you* joined our group. You were so *alive*, Katrina! I knew that you had died, because I thought about all the copies of our family letter that we had sent out, and the cards that came in response saying, "We are so sorry for the loss of your lovely daughter, Katrina." Then you were there…I don't remember talking about what happened, but I began to understand that you were still alive because your suicide attempt was just that – an attempt. Not a success. So you had gone away and didn't plan to

145

come home; you felt so guilty for what you tried to do.

We were all saying goodbye, taking pictures of each other – that sort of thing. And I came to you and gave you a hug. "God, I have wanted so much to hug Katrina one more time. For four months I have wanted this. And you let me! Thank you, thank you, *thank you*, dear Jesus. What a precious gift." As I wrapped my arms around Katrina, we both began to cry, she from sadness for having hurt me, and I from the joy of seeing her alive again. Oh, I know it was only a dream. But dreams and memories are all I have now, so they take the place of reality sometimes.

"Dear Lord, how I miss her. Will you come soon and take me Home? How I long to be with my Savior and sister."

Mar. 6

Keats wrote "Ode to A Nightingale" only a few months after his brother's death. The third stanza captures so well the longing of those who lose someone dear – they desire a place of refuge from their sorrow: "Forlorn! The very word is like a bell/To toll me back from thee to my sole self!"

Yes, I have joy – often and often – but I also have sorrow. I feel sad about the injustices of a world where sisters are separated in girlhood by death. I feel sorry for my sole self. Was it Job who said, "When can I go and be with God?" I don't remember, yet I echo the question now…

Mar. 22

In November or December, I found it so hard to limit my entries to two pages. Now I wonder how I'm supposed to fill even one page… what do I say that I have not already said?

Yet when I finish this letter-book to you, I will not close the door on my grief and say, "Well, it's all written down. I can go on with life now." No, I will keep writing about you and me and this unexpected journey through the land of the shadow.

Three days ago, we all remembered that it has been five months now… I couldn't help remembering when I saw "Mar. 19" on my calendar. I shudder mentally very time I see the number 19. I am not superstitious, but I can't help connecting that number to you and how old you were on the day you left us. I *do not* want to be 19.

I'm out of room. Goodbye for now, dearest Katrina… and yet, it's not "goodbye," but "see you later."

Eleven

It Is Sound
Where we are now

Crowds gathered each week to hear the soul-stirring sermons of Joseph Parker, the famous pastor of London's City Temple in the late 19th century. Then a crisis hit him hard. His wife died after an agonizing illness. Parker later said he would not have allowed a dog to suffer as she did. A heartbroken husband whose prayers had gone unanswered, he confessed publicly that for a week he had even denied that God existed.

But Parker's loss of faith was only temporary. From that experience he gained a stronger personal trust in Jesus' death-destroying resurrection and began to testify: "I have touched the bottom, and it is sound." Vernon C. Grounds, *Our Daily Bread*

• • •

In the aftermath of Katrina's death, my family and I have found this to be true in our own lives: We "have touched the bottom, and it is sound." We experienced a number of other painful separations and uprootings in the immediate months following, which were difficult to work through on top of our heavy grief over Katrina. Eventually, we found ourselves surrounded by a group of Christians who accepted us in our brokenness. Their love and encouragement helped us, especially my parents, find healing. My brother David, sister Rebecca, and I met our future spouses in this church fellowship.

In the Bible, Joseph tells his brothers, "You intended to harm me, but God intended it for good to accomplish what is now being done, the saving of many lives." (Gen. 50:20) Satan's lies harmed Katrina and brought her down. But we have watched in awe as God has brought beauty from the ashes of her death. We have all shared Katrina's story countless times, and God has used it in other lives (and repeatedly in my own life) as a message of truth, warning, and hope.

Because of Katrina's story, a girl told her parents about her anorexia and found healing that continues today. A young man on the verge of suicide walked away from death because he remembered the grief Katrina caused us. A man on the other side of the globe

147

came to Christ. A college friend of Katrina's chose a different career so that he could "reach out to teens who, like Katrina and I both, had struggles transitioning in life." The coroner who confirmed Katrina's suicide is a Christian and teaches a crisis intervention college course in which he shares her story. Katrina's first roommate, Amber, started an education course on suicide at Indiana University, where she was attending when Katrina died. While there, Amber says, "My roommate came to me in tears and told me that she was bulimic. I felt better prepared and more comfortable with the situation." Many people with struggles like Katrina's have been strengthened to keep fighting and not give in to Satan's deception. Others find help in supporting the "Katrina's" they know, or in comforting suicide survivors.

My parents took a counseling course to become better-equipped support for the hurting people God has brought into their lives. For four summers, they also hosted an amazing week-long Katrina School of Art at their farmhouse, which drew people from all over North America. Every person who attended had heard Katrina's story before coming and could relate to it in some way, which partly accounts for the depth of relationship that was built among them and my parents. Daddy and Mama have always had such big hearts for others, and the loss of Katrina expanded their love even more. By His incredible grace, their marriage has survived the crucible of losing their daughter. After several years as empty nesters, they sold their share of the farm, and moved across the border to live near Rebecca and me and our families.

I still can't get over God's gift of such a wise, understanding guy as my life companion. Like Professor Bhaer in the story of *Little Women*, Jesse came into the picture after Katrina (my Beth) died, and he has asked many questions about her, read several of her journals, and held me while I sobbed for her. He is eager to meet her someday. I couldn't have done this book without him.

Sunny southern Alberta, Canada, is home for us. We rent a house on an acreage next to Jesse's family and are just over an hour's drive from the farm where Katrina and I grew up. Between local handyman jobs with his brother, Jesse spends a lot of time studying for various teaching engagements and writing for our website. He says he fell completely in love with me when I riddled one of his essays with red ink, and he likes my work so much that I am still his editor and fellow book/idea-discusser today. He is always challenging and refreshing my mind and spirit as he ponders who we are, who God is, and what Christianity means.

Our passions have combined in great ways, and together we have developed a heart for reaching out to others, especially young people, with messages about the reality of Jesus Christ and how that affects their addictions, self image, and romantic relationships.

We have a growing family. Can't say how many kids we have, because, Lord willing, there'll be more by the time you read this. These children are priceless, incredibly stretching, and fill my heart to overflowing. I can't imagine life without them or their father. More than anything else, Jesse and our children have helped to close over the wound Katrina's death left inside me.

> But who shall so forecast the years
> And find in loss a gain to match?
> Or reach a hand through time to catch
> The far-off interest of tears?
> *In Memoriam*, Tennyson

Many of the great things that blossomed in my life and in others happened because God allowed me to hit the very bottom. There, like the preacher Joseph Parker, I have been discovering stronger faith in a more real, more wonderful God. I'm humbled to watch this Master Artist transform ashes into things of beauty. He is my greatest and only refuge. All praise goes to Him.

Twelve

On Depression

by Shaina Carter

Shaina and Katrina used to be pen pals when they were young. When Shaina and I reconnected in 2012, she read my book and sent me some of her own story, graciously allowing me to include it here. I believe her insights into suicidal thinking and depression can greatly help others who struggle with the same things, and also provide guidance for those supporting the suicidal and depressed.

Shaina's story is followed by a question and answer conversation between her and me.

Shaina:

I am sitting here in the dark with my heart completely wrung dry with guilt...that I am alive and Katrina is not. I have felt this survivor's guilt before, but never so acutely as now.

I remember hearing of Katrina's death while I was in a very deep pit of my own, when I had run away to Calgary to escape my pain and found that it followed me. I remember my mom asking me, "Shaina, you are not feeling so badly as Katrina, are you?" and telling her no, just like Katrina told her mom she wouldn't ever really commit suicide. I could hear the fear in my mom's voice and didn't want to be responsible for causing more pain, so I lied. Oh, the lies and deception that become your life when you are that devoured by despair.

In this book, Heidi questions the things that Katrina said in her suicide note that weren't true...the previous attempts, the journals never found...there are so many lies woven into the life of depression that you begin to believe them. You believe your own lies and half-truths and your mind becomes so confused, so mis-wired, so wrong that there is no way to decipher the truth even within yourself. I got to the point where I couldn't even decide what I wanted to eat from a menu because I no longer knew what I liked or disliked.

I know that suicide is often called "the coward's way out", but having tried it twice myself, I can tell you that isn't so. I honestly believed, and it sounds like Katrina did too, that if we removed ourselves and our sins from the lives of those we loved, they would be better off without us after a time of healing. It is completely wrong, but it is true in our mind at the time. I saw the effect I was having on my family and I wanted so much to stop hurting them. To stop being their constant worry and the reason my mom cried all the time. Yes, there was an element of wanting to escape my own pain, but the driving force was releasing my family from what I saw myself subjecting them to.

I used to pray very blatantly, "God, if I don't make it and I died or take my life, please, please, please use my death or my life to stop someone from feeling this despair."

Hearing my mom describe what it was like to talk to Katrina's mom after Katrina went home was one of the first thoughts to register in my mind that maybe suicide was not the right way. It is also important to remember that a person with severe depression and/or suicidal is *not* capable of completely rational thought. They are very ill and very desperate.

I see the darkness and evilness of the world much more than I ever did before I was raped at age sixteen and sank into nine years of hell on earth. And though I see this darkness and evil pressing in around us, I see God so much more clearly too.

I had one night where I longed so badly to die because I could see winged beings circling in my room, coming closer, and they were drenched in so much evil and hatred that I knew they wanted me to die. I don't know if I was hallucinating or if they were really there, but that's irrelevant. My fear was very real. To close my eyes would have been to allow them free access to my soul, I felt. I had not talked to God in years at that point except to scream obscenities at Him and accuse Him of not loving me.

That night, as evil circled me, I raged into the darkness and told God that I needed Him to do something because I could do nothing and I couldn't take anymore. Then I closed my eyes. I could feel the air moving around me and I truly believe a battle took place - is always taking place between good and evil.

Then a silence and a heavy weight of peace settled onto me and I knew my God again. It was not a miraculous change; I struggled for several more years after that, but I could no longer deny God's presence.

Heidi: So you started the slow journey to healing by going to God?

Shaina: I wear a ring that has the inscription "Live With Grace". We always talk about God pouring out His grace onto us, and He does, but I feel that Christians need to learn how to live *with* His grace. When you live with another person, there are inevitably times where you don't like them around, you are angry with them, annoyed, frustrated, disappointed and sad, but you know that if you acknowledge your feelings, share them, and put them in their place you will eventually return to loving and living in peace and contentment with the other person. And that it is a cycle. God's grace can cause those feelings in someone who is depressed because they *do* grasp God's grace, but they don't believe they deserve it and their unhappiness seems proof that since they don't deserve it they aren't receiving it. It is not until we dig right into grace, live in the filth of our sin and failings and how very utterly undeserving we are, accept our undeserving nature as the *reason* for grace, that we can begin to see the beauty of God's grace again. You must live *with* it to truly learn it and truly accept it. There is truth in the saying that you must hit rock bottom before you can start to come back up. I hit rock bottom three times, but I have learned to live with grace and to hang on to it as my life preserver.

Heidi: What about the claim that depression is simply a lack of faith?

Shaina: Those who are depressed do not so much need advice as unending love and we must be the conduits of that when they cannot feel God. I feel very strongly that the Christian community has done a disservice to people struggling with depression by promoting the belief that if they could "have more faith," they will be healed. Depression can be so crippling, and the guilt and shame the person feels so overwhelming, that they do not have the capability to pray and seek God and build their faith. Sometimes the groaning of the soul that the Spirit carries to God for us is the only communication we can manage. Depression is the strangest mix of complete lack of feeling and utter anguish. It's hard to explain how that feels to someone who hasn't stood at the gates to the valley of death.

I believe that King David was truly depressed. Psalms, in my Bible, is full of my scribbling, underlining, highlighting, and crying out to God. I believe books like Psalms are there to teach us both how to express our despair and anger to God, as well as our repentance, joy and fulfillment. We find it so hard to rail at God because we feel guilty, as if we should only be praising Him, but

God desires a real relationship with us and a real relationship requires the honest expression of disappointment, anger, and sadness as well. We need to teach people that God is big enough to handle our anger, resentment, and disappointment in Him. And when we do that, we begin to let Him in again. Once we let Him back in, we can begin to feel His love and grace again.

Heidi: You said you had to make the choice to recover from depression. What did that look like?

Shaina: The first step that was crucial was accepting I was sick. I don't think it is healthy or necessary to say, "I am depressed."

I found it more helpful to say, "I have depression." When a person has cancer they don't say "I am cancer."

They say, "I have cancer." There seems to be a fundamental inclination to make depression a personal attribute of the person, when, in fact, it is an illness like any other. But anyhow, accepting that I had depression was the all important first step.

The second step was deciding that I was going to manage it. Depression is extremely good at stripping you of any sense of ability or strength. You feel immensely weak, useless, helpless, and despair is the prevalent feeling. I had to make a conscious choice to learn how to control its effect on my life.

Thirdly, I sat down with my family and my closest friends/mentors and talked to them about what I was going through. It's very difficult to explain how you feel to someone who is not depressed. There has to be understanding on *both* sides that there will never be complete understanding. I didn't have anyone to talk to who had experienced depression.

I told my family and friends what it was like to live inside my brain. How crippling and lonely it was. How sad, black, hopeless and ugly it was. I was very raw with them, explaining that it was possible to feel absolutely nothing and feel horrible for feeling nothing at the same time. This was especially true regarding my family. I often felt completely separate from them, even when I was with them. They could all be talking, laughing, including me and loving me and I would feel apart, lonely, and numb inside.

I also told them that when I *did* know what I needed, there were things they could do. They could listen, they could distract me, they could get me out of the house, they could come and stay with me, they could give advice, they could not give advice. I told them that sometimes they would get it wrong and that it was ok. I gave them permission to fail at helping me and they gave me permission to be very vocal with them about what I needed. I explained there were times that I didn't know what I needed and that if they felt up to trying to figure it out, I would be accepting of that.

I apologized in advance for the days when I did not receive their love and help well, and asked for their patience. There were a lot of times when I did not know what I needed, and I know that a lot of people who loved me suffered through their poorly received attempts at helping me.

Sometimes they would just sit with me and pray with me when I had no words to pray. My mom was there for me without question and listened to me talk about the same miseries over and over and over...and then would make me get out of the house for a walk where we only talked about other things.

Heidi: Earlier, you touched on the emotional deadness you felt. How did you fight that?

Shaina: I think my family often knew I was "faking" my happiness, but I don't really feel it was wrong of me to fake it. It wasn't really faking, it was more acting on my half of the relationship with them. I knew they loved me, I knew that I loved them, I knew I didn't feel it at the moment, and I knew that it was my responsibility to express it to them anyway. It is like our relationship with God; we don't always feel close to Him or feel like talking to Him, but it is still necessary that we talk to Him and seek Him.

Heidi: What about the days you tried the things you just mentioned and still were not able to function?

Shaina: It was very important to allow myself to fail. I worked at many small goals on my journey to getting better: Could I get out of bed, could I make it to work, could I get through the day without crying? All these things seem so inconsequential when you're healthy, but when you are not, they are sometimes monumental. When you fail at those little things, it's very easy to sink back into depression and stop trying. That's when the hopelessness creeps back in. But when you fail at one of those things, it's more helpful to say "Okay, I did not reach that goal right now, but I can try again later." We are human and we fail, and learning to emerge from depression

155

is one of the hardest things I've ever experienced. We have to be forgiving of ourselves as well. It is very much about retraining your brain and thought patterns.

Heidi: What other treatment helped you? Did you try antidepressants?

Shaina: Treatment is a huge topic, but I'm happy to share what I found worked for me, and also that I believe a combination of treatments is best.

First off, yes, I was on antidepressants over the years. I was on and off several different ones as it takes a while to find one that works for you. People don't react the same way to every medication. I found some completely useless and ineffective, some just gave me side effects, and one helped save my life.

As I've mentioned before, depression clouds your thinking and rewires your brain to work along dysfunctional lines. When that happens to an extreme degree (as with me), it's almost impossible to retrain your own brain and make the changes necessary to get better. I found that antidepressants alleviated my depression enough that I could think as clearly as I needed to, to retrain my brain. Antidepressants brought me away from the brink of suicide where I had been twice before.

I strongly believe that antidepressants in combination with therapy is the most effective treatment. The antidepressants manage the symptoms so that you can learn from your therapist, and so that you can see your "mis-thoughts", as it were, enough to change them.

Remember, my brain was so clouded that I couldn't even figure out what I wanted to eat from a menu, let alone realize that thoughts such as, "I am so horrible that I bet my family would actually be happy if I died" were ridiculous. As the extreme thoughts, overwhelming sadness, and fears dimmed with medication, I was able to pinpoint with my therapist, friends, and family the things I needed to change.

Without medication I don't think I would have been successful in therapy, and without therapy I would have simply been a dulled down version of my depressed self. Therapy is extremely important because it provides a non-biased, trained, professional opinion from someone who knows how to teach you the tricks that will overcome depression.

I still use a lot of the tricks I learned in therapy when I feel that I am sliding towards a little bit of depression again. I can easily identify incorrect thoughts and feelings, and have the tools needed to deal with them effectively.

I am no longer on medication and haven't been for seven years. I was twenty-five when I made the decision to heal, and it was about a year after that, that I felt in control enough to be slowly taken off medication, under the supervision of my doctor and my therapist. I don't need a therapist or medication any more, I'm happy to say.

It is true, sadly, that in a lot of faith circles, sickness (especially mental) is viewed as spiritual judgment. This makes me more angry than anything. Do we really think our mental capabilities are so incredible that any lack in them is judgment from God? Or lack of faith? Our bodies, our minds, our souls, our hearts...*all* are fallible. *All* can be ill and need healing. I do *not* believe God punishes us through mental illness nor physical illness.

Mental illness is just one more symptom of our fallenness, just the same as anything else. God wants to heal it just like He wants to heal our physical illnesses - and sometimes He doesn't heal - but I believe He wants us to seek help and treatment. He gave us the ability to develop medicine, and therapy and counseling for a reason and that reason is to minister to one another for His glory.

Heidi: I can tend to be pretty negative; that trait runs in our family. I'm not sure why, but it's very real and prevalent, and I wonder if this contributed to Katrina's hopelessness.

Shaina: Oh, yes, it is very real and prevalent. There is a very strong genetic factor to depression. My dad, his mom, and my mom's dad all suffered depression as well. I think I have had a stronger streak than some because of the trauma I experienced when I was raped at age sixteen, but it is definitely genetically encoded in me to tend toward depression.

I am glad you can recognize it in yourself and your family. Denial is very unhealthy. Those traits can definitely be high-jacked by the thought patterns that depression breeds. It is good to be aware of them and be proactive in changing them. God doesn't ask us to worry. In fact, he commands us *not* to worry. It's hard, but it is worth working at.

Heidi: Your family and friends were helped hugely by your sitting

157

them down and laying it all out for them. Not everyone does that, though.

Shaina: I wish everyone could do this. It took me years and years to. One of the reasons I found it so hard to talk to them was that I had so successfully shut them out and driven a wedge between me and them. I really hadn't wanted their help and told them so (to my shame) so many times that I can't blame them for not pushing me more. It also made it a lot harder to humble myself and say, "Yes, I do actually want your help now."

Some people are not at a place where they feel comfortable doing that, or simply don't feel equipped to. Unfortunately, no one can force them to speak out. Again, I suggest offering concrete suggestions of things you could do, or just being quiet and listening. Sometimes after asking me something, some people have answered their own questions, when I just waited a bit and gave them time to think.

Heidi: Some people say there is no guaranteed life preserver for my depressed friend, no way of knowing whether she will get better.

Shaina: Depression has some overarching characteristics: sadness, hopelessness, apathy, lack of motivation, loss of desires and enjoyment of things and life, anger, numbness...but it is also particular to each person.

What I share are just the thoughts and emotions of one person. My story is definitely different from other people's. For me, recovering from depression was a choice and the most difficult one I have ever had to make. Sometimes your friend will need to make the choice daily, hourly, sometimes by the minute. Rejoice over every little conquest of choice and do not wallow in the constant human failures that we all make.

I sometimes have seasons in my life where I am down or depressed, and I suppose it is possible that I could become suicidally depressed again at some point, but I don't think I will. I made the choice to recover, and the success of that choice will be what I will use to battle any slips towards depression now and in the future. I have built a foundation now.

Heidi: For a practical person like me who wants to jump in and shoulder burdens so my friend can rest lighter, it is hard not to do more than listening and praying.

Shaina: While we all want to "help" someone with depression by doing things for them, you have to be careful not to do too much. Most people with depression feel a distinct lack of ability and skill. Your friend will likely feel as if she isn't good at anything and isn't capable of things she previously was more than capable of doing. The more you do those things for her, the more you feed her feelings of inadequacy and apathy. Holding a depressed person to her responsibilities is actually very important in helping her get better. Otherwise you are increasing her feeling of not being useful, wanted, needed. You increase her feeling that everyone could get along just fine without her.

When I hit rock bottom, my mom came to get me and brought me home. I had lived on my own for five years already and it was difficult for me. I stayed with them just over a year and spent the first three months sleeping, crying, and exhausting myself and my parents with talk. Wisely, they recognized the right time for me to start getting up and doing things. They started giving me more responsibilities and raised their expectations of me. I ended up going back to school for the year and that was incredibly helpful.

Everyone's time frame will look different, but it is very unhealthy for people to take over most or all of the responsibilities of a person with depression for too long of a time. It is imperative that they start taking control of their own life again and re-assuming their responsibilities. How else will they regain their sense of accomplishment and capability? Also, there is incredible power in maintaining normalcy in life.

Heidi: I hesitate to share about my daily life with my friend, thinking that it'll just painfully highlight her own unhappiness. I'm healthy and have a happy life, and so of course I can crank out my gratitude for life's blessings.

Shaina: Helping someone with depression is probably one of the most frustrating experiences a person can undertake. You are right, it is very possible for your words of joy, encouragement and advice to cause pain. You are also right that the simple fact that you are happy and joyful could hurt a depressed person. But *do not* think that means you have no right to experience or share those things.

Also, a good way to temper inundating her with your joy and

159

making her feel worse, is to also relay things you struggle with and ask her for prayer. This does many things: makes her feel needed, makes her feel like you consider her prayer and advice as valid and wanted, and helps to bring her out of herself a bit as well. I can't stress enough how making a depressed person feel they are needed and wanted is so incredibly key to helping them.

Heidi: I am so aware that attempts to help a depressed friend can be and are misconstrued, and wind up hurting more than helping.

Shaina: This is unavoidable, unfortunately. You are not responsible for the reactions to your efforts to help; all you can do is observe how your friend reacts and learn from it. You can also encourage her to tell you how she needs help. Sometimes, you could ask her if one of a few options would be helpful: can I pray for you, make some phone calls for you, shut up and listen, distract you? etc. Don't give too many options (people with depression often struggle to make the simplest of decisions), but if you give her a few, she can choose from them, or choose none of them, or it might help her to think of something else she might need.

It's probably hard for your depressed friend to acknowledge that she feels no joy in things she previously did, especially when it concerns how she feels about your family, kids, etc. It causes a lot of guilt and grief to experience that lack of feeling. I would encourage her to write down the moments of joy every day, even if there is only one and it only lasted five seconds, and even if it takes her an hour of thinking to come up with it, and even if it's only that she had one moment where she simply felt normal...not happy, or wonderful, or joyful, just normal.

Heidi: Like you said, though one who is depressed often feels dead emotionally, she can also be very sensitive. I don't wish to add pain. It seems like many attempts to reach out and love might look like hand grenades lobbed at her. Yet on the other hand, it's kind of insulting to her, isn't it, to assume she'll be so hurt by my efforts to help?

Shaina: While it isn't insulting to assume she will be hurt (because yes, we are very easily hurt), it doesn't mean you should stop attempting to help. It's almost unavoidable to cause pain or feel confused. You will most likely "add pain" at some point, but not usually because of something you have done or said, but more because the other person is hypersensitive and unable to process things with any sort of equilibrium. Spend extra time thinking about how to phrase things with love, but don't feel you have to wear kid gloves with everything you say. Sometimes we need to hear the hard truths, if they are spoken in love.

Heidi: What did people do or not do that hurt you most?

Shaina: I was far more hurt by the people who held constant silence than those who tried and sometimes failed to help me. Though I fully admit I pushed them away aggressively, I was disappointed in those who held back and held their tongues so much. It was my non-Christian friends who insisted on pushing into my darkness that kept me alive during my darkest years. They literally took knives out of my apartment, forced me to go the emergency room, and physically chased me down the street when I was completely panicking and wanting to run into traffic.

I am not exaggerating for effect. Those were hideously real moments in my life and I owe my life to God using non-Christians to keep me alive. Meanwhile, the Christians kept mostly silent. There are a lot of psychologists and experts who tell you not to try to force someone with depression to get help, and that is true...but you can insist on being present in their lives, *with love*. The friends who were removing knives and chasing me down the street never once said to me, "You're crazy, what is wrong with you? Why don't you get help?"

They all said, "We are scared for you, we love you, we aren't going away easily, and we want to help you get help."

It was only by God's grace and love that He sent in non-Christians, knowing that I was completely unreceptive to him or Christians at that time. In no way do I blame the people who held silence during that time for making me worse, nor do I hold a grudge. In fact, many of them, including my family, were very instrumental in my healing once I finally opened up to them. For a long time, I did not let them in and they didn't know how to find a way in. It's sadly a very common situation.

I would strongly encourage every person, Christian or not, to be a visible and tangible presence in the life of someone with depression. Don't wait and don't hesitate. Expect to be rebuffed and go in armed with prayer and every shred of love you can find in your heart. Perhaps you will be the voice that is heard.

Heidi: We've talked about the emotional and spiritual pain of depression. Can you tell me about the physical pain?

Shaina: I still struggle with times of depression, and the first thing I notice is *not* my mood, but my physical reactions. I get swollen glands in my neck, start sleeping more, and feel slightly nauseous. Sometimes my skin feels extra itchy and I feel generally unwell. I have been watching myself and my reactions for a long time, and I know these are signs of depression creeping in and not a cold or flu.

It sounds crazy, yes, but it is true. The physical symptoms of depression are very well documented. I understand pain as well, as I have had migraines for well over ten years and have had chronic back/neck pain since my car accident five years ago. These things can trigger my depression, and my depression can make these things worse. I choose to deal with each as they come and manage myself. It *does* work.

I would encourage your depressed friend to attempt to separate her physical pain from her mental pain. This is where looking for joy moments can come in: seeking relief from mental pain even if the physical pain cannot be stopped.

Heidi: When did you start to feel like you were turning the corner toward a sort of normal again?

Shaina: The day I truly started to heal was the day I decided that I was going to learn to "manage" my depression and not "get rid of it." I didn't really set out to "get better", but set out to manage my depression and learn how to live within it. I had come to a point where I felt that I was going to be ill forever and wanted to simply learn how to live with it, manage it, and discover how to let it be something that God could use. I never wanted to be at the point of suicide again, and really, at first my goal was just not to sink that low.

God is a God who can heal, but He is also a God who places thorns in our sides. When I finally prayed, "God, please let me learn to manage my depression so that I can be used for the furthering of Your kingdom whether I am healthy or not," that was when I started to heal.

I can't tell you why we suffer such a darkness as depression and I can't explain why some people can heal from it and others can't. I certainly had no greater faith than Katrina did when she went home. I don't know why I was allowed to continue stumbling after God.

I will carry my survivor's guilt with me to the end, but I think that this is a good thing. It constantly reminds me that every stitch of God's grace is more than I deserve. That though He promises joy, He also promises suffering and sorrow. My life, though mostly free of depression now, has left me living as raw as an exposed nerve ending, acutely aware of those around me who are suffering.

I would not trade that sensitivity for anything.

Thirteen

If I Had a Second Chance

Open letters from Daddy and Mama

By Loraine Wahl

May 2014

Oh, my precious Katrina, if only I could have known then what I know now. If I could rewind history, my response to you would be different. If only I could once again put my arm around you and look into your eyes with compassion, I would speak into your life words of hope and encouragement. If only you knew that freedom from your eating habits was within reach, and that you had everything you needed for life and godliness.

Let me share a bit of my own story with you… First, let me fix your favorite cup of hot tea, and then we'll find a comfy corner to sit and chat, okay?

When I was fifteen, only three years younger than you are now, I developed a problem with eating. No, I wasn't sick. Life was good. Being the third oldest of seven, with a mother who took her role as homemaker very seriously and a father who worked hard to provide for us, I really had nothing to complain about. Except that my dad wasn't home much; he was so involved with his job, as well as in the church and the community. Our family had a good name in our area. Sadly, I didn't get to know my father like you know your own Daddy. Anyhow, I was an A-student in a rural public school on central Vancouver Island. All my spare time at school and much of it at home was taken up with studying and practicing piano and trying to do it all just right. In fact, on Awards Day at the end of Grade 10, I received an engraved trophy for the highest marks in my grade level. I had always been a very shy, independent sort of girl, and longed to please my teachers and everyone around me.

Somewhere along the way, and I don't know what triggered it, I began eating less. Television and Barbie dolls were nonexistent in our home, so their influence couldn't be to blame. Losing weight felt satisfying. Subconsciously, my thoughts focused more and more on myself. My mom became worried that I wasn't eating normally at mealtimes, but little did she know that I was sneaking raisins or other forbidden snacks in between meals. Naturally, I felt guilty, but what should I do? I was such a compliant child and feared any inkling of punishment if I dared to own up to my senseless habits. The dozens of Bible verses I had memorized to earn my way to Bible Camp were the furthest thing from my mind. I honestly didn't know how Scripture could be practical in my secret struggle.

I recall saving a year's worth of my allowance money so that I could buy a train ticket to Ontario in the summer to pick fruit with my cousin. I lived with my aunt and uncle, whom I grew to love so much. We didn't discuss my food issues. They just smothered me with love and encouragement. I remember returning home to the Island after those two wonderful months, with cash in my pocket.

My memory is a bit fuzzy now, but something gradually changed afterwards, and in hindsight, I realized that I wasn't as immersed in myself as I had been prior to that summer. But then my eating habits flip-flopped, and right on into my early college years, I struggled with keeping my weight in balance. Countless times, I was so frustrated at myself for lacking self-control. What I thought would provide satisfaction, namely food, became an obsession. I was worshiping the creation, meaning food, weight, approval of others, and not the Creator. What precious time I had wasted!

I am grateful that over a long period of time God delivered me from this destructive pattern of enslavement, to worshiping my Savior. I realize now that His grace and His incredible love for me brought me back on track.

Sweetheart, you seem surprised at what I just shared with you. That's okay. I should have told you this story much sooner. Just like you poured out your heart in the journal entry you placed on our bed that evening, I felt you needed to know that you're not in this alone. I understand. Your cry for help was sincere and I realized that I desperately needed God's wisdom to know how to help you. In my teen years, I didn't know how to ask for His wisdom, let alone help from anyone else. How about if we ask for wisdom right now?

O God, thank you that you are keenly interested in every part of Katrina's life. You know how heavy her burden is right now and so I beg for your wisdom. I ask in faith, believing that you will not allow her to waste this trial, but that through it, her walk with you will become so much stronger and deeper. Give me wisdom to know when to speak and when to be silent. In your holy name, Amen.

Katrina, when you were just a little girl, you would

sometimes come running to me and say, "Mama, I need a hug." All you needed was the assurance that someone loves you and understands. That warm embrace gave you the hope you needed to get through the day. In the same way, your Heavenly Father wants you, as His child, to come running to Him. He wants to embrace you with His love and give you hope. He is compassionate and personal. He wants to be in the center of your suffering, the counselor in the midst of your confusion and hopelessness. You can trust Him to keep His promises.

At age four, when you gave your heart to Jesus, you believed with genuine, childlike faith that God rescued you from the consequences of sin. Today, His grace is just as available to you as it was then. In your journal entry, you mentioned your never-ending cycle of sin-repentance-forgiveness, and so on. Someone once told me that sin is what we do when we're not satisfied with God. Would that be the same as saying that your food habits are like a cult that tries to manage life apart from God? It feels like such a hopeless, lonesome road that leads to nowhere. But God's rich grace is much greater than your sin, and the Holy Spirit living in you will give you the power to have victory over that sin. Remember, God doesn't love you based on your performance. Just think, you are one of the sheep He has called by name, and He will not condemn you. I don't doubt for a minute that you desperately want to change. Your willingness to change is a huge step in the right direction, Katrina. Would you like to pray and ask God to forgive you for your sin of despair, selfishness, pride, and unbelief, and then ask Him to begin changing your attitude and thought patterns? Let's both kneel down and pray.

Amen!

In your journal, I sense that you often feel like a failure. Am I right? When I mess up, I can't believe that I actually did that bad thing, and it's hard on my pride. A pity party would seem like the best option. But is God pleased when we wallow in our failure? No. Failure isn't final. He wants you and me to confess it and press forward. I'm not saying this is easy, but I can say that joy and a willing spirit come from genuinely making an effort to please God, and not please myself or others. To put it into clearer perspective, ask yourself "Am I motivated by my desire to please God or by the fear of failure?" There *is* a way of escape. There *is* hope! Why? Because God *is* faithful.

How about a tea refill? Or a bowl of fresh nectarine slices?

167

Oh, and if you have anything to ask or add, please feel free to interject.

To continue where I left off... When you've given up all hope, when you feel like an utter failure, God gives a guarantee in His Word. I've noted it in my Bible, as I often do when I hear or read something that casts light on a verse. To personalize that guarantee, I'll insert your name: *Based upon My (God's) own faithfulness, i.e., upon the integrity of My own Word and Person, I declare that there is no problem or trial that My redeemed daughter, Katrina, will ever face anything that is either unique or beyond her ability to handle if she meets the problem in My way, using My resources.* Notice, God said *no* problem. That includes your food idol.

But first, your attitude toward your problem must change radically. A hopeful attitude will reap positive results. Let me give you an example. Okay, you're a first-class pianist. How did you get to that level? By gradually, day by day, year by year, working toward the goals that I and your other piano teachers set for you, right? Sometimes you felt like closing the books and giving up, but when you changed your attitude and hope prevailed, you reached the goals, one by one. It took continued daily effort. The results didn't come overnight, as much as you sometimes wished they would. From mastering *The Old Mill Wheel* at the beginner level, to performing Chopin's *Nocturne in C-Sharp Minor*, you can see that there was growth and change in the way you approached the piano keys. And the results were absolutely beautiful!

Likewise, in your eating habits, it will take effort and time to change, like you said in your journal. There's no quick, easy way. It's like learning to crawl, then taking baby steps, then walking, and finally running. You'll fall a few times along the way and want to give up. Because the Holy Spirit dwells in you, He will give you the power to discard wrong habits and acquire lasting new habits that please God. And He promises to give you the grace and courage to rise above each challenge, if you allow Him to. The "can-do" heart believes the truth that God gives us all things necessary for life and godliness, and the "I can't" heart believes the lie that "I can't do this anymore," thereby doubting God's promise that He will make a way of escape. Just as surely as you made a wrong turn in your eating patterns, it is just as certain that there will be a way out. Isn't it reassuring to know you can continue to assume your responsibilities before God? That spells *hope* for change and growth!

Lasting lifestyle change at the heart level is possible when we take the Bible seriously. God's Book is very practical. It's about what life is about, and speaks to dealing with temptations, fears, selfishness, despair, and thought patterns. It speaks compassionately to you with Jesus' words, "(Katrina), let not your heart (mind, emotions, will) be troubled; believe in God, believe also in Me." Sweetheart, it's not a sin to have a heavy heart; Jesus Himself was troubled when He faced the Cross. But it is what you do with that troubled heart that will either break you or set you free. Katrina, when you fix your eyes on Jesus and see His goodness, your struggles with temptation will diminish, and your weary soul will have the strength to rise above despair. You will learn to endure in spite of failures.

Would you like to spend time with me every morning and evening, reading specific passages in Scripture about God's love and grace, His promises, and His commandments? Together, let's be surprised by who God really is, and then talk about it. Regardless of how you feel, if you use the Bible daily, it will discipline you, and in turn bring freedom from sin, and resulting joy. You've discovered that with piano playing, right? Daily, structured practice eventually produces more freedom in your playing, doesn't it?

Waging war against sin also calls for obedience to what the Scriptures teach. *No matter how you feel.* Feeling-oriented living is a major hindrance to becoming a godly young woman. You can learn to delight in obedience. Aggressively pursue godly living not just by avoiding sin but by hating it. I encourage you to be accountable to me or to one of your sisters so that in your weak moments you have someone to partner with and provide support.

In my own life, I'm learning that an attitude of thankfulness goes a long way toward working through difficult situations. The Psalms is loaded with reminders for us to have a grateful heart, especially when the burdens of life get us down. To start with, when you awaken in the morning, before you do anything else, make it a habit to speak these words aloud: "Good morning, Lord, and thank you for the promise of another day. Please show me what I can do to serve you today. Give me a grateful heart and help me to expect great things from you. Thank you that I can trust you."

I find that when I express my waking thoughts in this manner of gratitude to God, a brighter tone greets the rest of the day. Next, look for at least one thing during the day that you can be thankful for, and gradually increase the number. Be specific.

Replace your negative thinking with praiseworthy thinking. I'll be on your team, and at day's end, we'll share our joys with each other, okay?

When Hannah of the Old Testament fell into hopelessness and despair because she couldn't bear a child, she took her burden to the Lord by crying out to Him. Your burdens, Katrina, can bring you to a deeper place in prayer, when you unload your heart to your Heavenly Father. He promises to sustain you and carry you. Try to see every jolt in your life's journey as an opportunity to grow in your faith. God does not waste anything. Don't give up trying just because it got hard. Jesus must become your first love again, and the only way you can learn to love Him is to know Him from the Bible. Because I love you and care deeply about you, I'm available to come alongside and help you walk this path to freedom and peace. During our time in the Word each day, let's also pray together, okay?

If only...

I could kneel down with you next to me, lovingly put my arm around you, and pray with you, my precious Katrina Suzanne, these words would pour from the depths of my heart:

Dear Heavenly Father, you are a God of love, and you care deeply about your children. I praise you that, at a young age, Katrina trusted in Christ's death and resurrection for her salvation. Thank you that you are trustworthy and keep all your promises. In Christ, she has been promised victory, and I ask now that you will give her the grace to claim victory and freedom from the sinful eating habits that are enslaving her. Draw her to yourself, and hear the cries of her heart, O God. Help her to learn who you really are and all that you have already done for her on the cross. By saturating her mind with biblical truth, I pray that her thinking patterns will change, and she will be able to stand strong against the Enemy's attacks. May she rest in your incredible love for her, and help her to obey your voice, through the Holy Spirit's prompting. Show me ways I can encourage and bless her each day. In Jesus' trustworthy name, Amen.

By Russ Wahl

May 2015

Dear Katrina,

In the days before the requirement of child car seats and while driving down the road, sometimes I would reach over and tickle one of you sitting beside me. I remember once, I tickled you a time or two as we drove home together. Then I put my hand on my lap and continued to drive. Soon I felt your little hand reach over to mine and bring it to your tummy – for another tickle. You had that quiet way, to get a tickle when you wanted it! How those days of raising you were filled with many joys and challenges.

Though you are not with us here on earth, your memory lingers, painfully and beautifully. Almost four years after you left us, hurricane Katrina struck the United States. It was the costliest natural disaster and was one of the five deadliest hurricanes in the history of the United States. Your name came up often in the news. At first, while still grieving, I dreaded hearing your name on the radio but as time went by, I found those announcements prompting me to remember you with joy.

Katrina, you were given very special gifts that I did not come to genuinely understand or fully appreciate. In time, as you grew older and expressed yourself more I saw just how special you were. In fact, now that you have been gone from us for over fourteen years, I find myself loving you more and being so grateful for the years we had with you. I am reminded of the saying that sometimes comes up after the eulogy is given at a funeral. "These things should have been said to him when he was alive." Or: "Give flowers when someone is alive not after they die." I think we don't because we become familiar. Familiarity may cause us to take one another for granted. I took you for granted too much, Katrina.

As I think back over the years and our time together, I realized that, if given the opportunity, I would do some things differently in raising you. Some people, in reading our story, might ask that nagging, painful question, "What went wrong?" In response I could sweep my pen with a very broad stroke and say: Adam and Eve went wrong. Original sin went wrong. And ... I went wrong. Looking back over my life, I see such a huge chasm of spiritual immaturity – even when I served the church as a leader and elder for years before you left us. It may appear an irony to some who know me that the older I get, the more of my failures, imperfections and frailties I see. Oh, it is the grace of God that sustains.

Katrina, you were a bit of a ruffian when you were little. We worked at teaching you to be gentle with your siblings. Besides that peculiar characteristic about you, you were, in your heart, a very sensitive little girl. I believe you held an intense desire to please God and pleasing God without a good, heartfelt understanding of the *rest* and the *joy* administered by His grace ultimately does not satisfy. I failed to read your heart very well and often fell into a "Do this and don't do that" obedience method of training instead of listening to you and frequently expressing love to you. I let the "tyranny of the urgent" – farm life, church life, "family life"- occupy more of my time. Did I notice that you were slowly and subtly shifting to a more legalistic, rules-following little girl? I didn't, though there were enough indications.

Our desire for you children was that you, equipped with the gospel, could influence many in your adult life for the kingdom. So we taught you to read, write and speak well. Our first desire was that you would marry, but felt that a college education would prepare you for employment in the event that your husband were to die and we were unable to support you and children. We also felt that a college education could help you mature and develop your mind for life later. They were not the best reasons for sending you off. The summer before you died we sent you to Summit with Heidi and then on a missions trip to the Philippines. Now I realize that it was too much for you. I just did not see it at the time. Your struggles in college, though well covered by "my little girl with her stiff upper lip", should have tipped me off to the very good idea, "Bring Katrina home." I struggled, "When does one determine that the process of the maturing that trials produce in a person is too much – or that it is okay to press on a little more?" Naturally, in your desire to please us you withheld expressing much of the pain you felt: of separation from us, of the intensity of your studies, your dietary struggles, etc. You were a highly talented young lady, yet a little girl inside who really had a longing to be home.

You were a perfectionist and, not like me, you could often reach those goals you set. Unfortunately your art projects could always be done "just a little better" which kept you out late at night to make it just right. And your bulimia was a struggle that you just could not win easily, this huge emotional, spiritual, and physical battle. Mama and I didn't realize what a monster it was to you until

172

too late.

If I could do it all over again, I'd have pushed myself very hard to learn all I could about grace, God's grace to me and His grace expressed through me to you. I'd have slowed down and listened to you and overlooked the feelings that the best for you was college and learning a skill. I'd have kept you home and given you the nurturing environment you needed to learn to rest in the completed work of Christ on the cross. But, you see, I too was unfamiliar with the beauty of a life lived in grace and the joy that passes understanding. In fact, I still struggle to grasp those powerfully beautiful gifts from God.

Some people might ask, "What went wrong?" To that I am not sure I can respond. As the years have passed, I have come to look at life itself in a very different way than when you were with us. Life in Christ here on earth, takes on a clearer focus and one that cannot be explained to others. Sometimes I feel like I am speaking a different language of the heart or that the eyes of my heart have been opened in a very small and subtle way.

So, "What went wrong?" Maybe a more accurate description of what I went through since you left might be, "What went right?" I could list the many blessings and depth of relationship with God and his children that have all risen out of the slough of those days of anguish and grief. I look at heaven with a much clearer understanding and yearn, with tears, for that precious home, my real home. I join the apostle John in his humble, longing plea, "Come, Lord Jesus." And I am so grateful for Jesus' promise "Yes, I am coming quickly." What a precious friend of sinners....

Sweetheart, soon God Himself will be among us. He will wipe away every tear from our eyes. He will take mourning and crying and pain away from us. I long for that. I desire Him. And, I yearn for you, my girl.

You are so beautifully precious to me, my Katrina.

173

Fourteen

Helps

If you feel like giving up on life:

Christian Suicide Prevention
Phone: 888-667-5947- 9 pm to 1 am (every night) and 11 am to 1 pm (Monday and Wednesday mornings) Central Time
E-mail: contact@christiansuicideprevention.com
www.christiansuicideprevention.com

Warning signs for suicide:
- **previous suicide attempts**
- **talking about dying**: any mention of dying (or desiring death), disappearing, jumping, shooting oneself, or other types of self-harm; suicidal impulses, statements, plans
- **loss of interest**: dropping out of activities previously enjoyed (sports, school, job)
- **change in personality**: A sudden elated mood following a time of depression; being unusually quiet or unusually aggressive/angry
- **change in behavior**: can't concentrate on school, work, routine tasks; agitation, hyperactivity, restlessness or lethargy
- **change in eating habits**: loss of appetite and weight, or overeating
- **fear of losing control**: going crazy, harming self or others
- **low self-esteem**: feeling worthless, shame, overwhelming guilt, self-hatred, "everyone would be better off without me"
- **risk-taking behavior**: e.g. reckless driving (speeding or running red lights)
- **no hope for future**: believing things will never get better; that nothing will ever change
- extravagant spending, giving away favorite things, visiting or calling people to say goodbye, making out wills, arranging for the care of pets
- substance abuse

Compiled from:
"Warning Signs: Recognize the Signs of Possible Suicide Risk"
(www.sfsuicide.org). Used by permission.
"Recognize the Warning Signs of Suicide" (www.webmd.com)

What to do if you know someone who has these symptoms:
- *Find a non-threatening way to express concern* about your friend's erratic behavior, feelings of failure, or obsession with death. If your friend has expressed any of these things to you, bring up those statements in your conversation. Ask for clarification. Communicate your sincere desire to help your friend, as well as your serious concern for his safety and well-being.
- *Ask him to promise not to do anything without talking to you first.* That promise can often help in moments of desperation.
- *Be available to talk* whenever your friend needs to vent. Oftentimes, a depressed and suicidal person can find a lot of emotional release and healing in verbalizing feelings, struggles, or fears. Simply by listening carefully to your friend, you can help him take strides toward normalcy by allowing him a safe place to work through different issues. While seeking to be compassionate and very sensitive toward your friend's pain, gently but firmly remind him of what is true not only about his situation in life, but also about God and the good purposes He has for his life. Ask him, "How do you think your suicide would affect your family and friends?" Urge your friend, as often as necessary, to seriously consider the impact his death would have on others. *Encourage him to begin seeing a Christian counselor* regularly to receive practical steps toward proper, healthy thinking and decision-making. Above all, *pray continually for God to give you wisdom* to know what truths to share with your friend.

What to do if you are suicidal:
- Promise not to do anything right now
Even though you're in a lot of pain right now, give yourself some distance between thoughts and action. Make a promise to yourself: "I will wait 24 hours and won't do anything drastic during that time." Or, wait a week. Thoughts and actions are two different things—your suicidal thoughts do not have to become a reality. There is no deadline, no one pushing you to act on these thoughts immediately. Wait. Wait and put some distance between your suicidal thoughts and suicidal action.
- Avoid drugs and alcohol
Suicidal thoughts can become even stronger if you have taken drugs or alcohol. It is important to not use non-prescription drugs or alcohol when you feel hopeless or are thinking about suicide.
- Make your home safe

Remove things you could use to hurt yourself, such as pills, knives, razors, or firearms. If you are unable to do so, go to a place where you can feel safe. If you are thinking of taking an overdose, give your medicines to someone who can return them to you one day at a time, or as you need them.

- Take hope—people *do* get through this

Even people who feel as badly as you are feeling now manage to survive these feelings. Take hope in this. There is a very good chance that you are going to live through these feelings, no matter how much self-loathing, hopelessness, or isolation you are currently experiencing. Just give yourself the time needed and don't try to go it alone.

- Don't keep these suicidal feelings to yourself

Many of us have found that the first step to coping with suicidal thoughts and feelings is to share them with someone we trust. It may be a friend, a therapist, a member of the clergy, a teacher, a family doctor, a coach, or an experienced counselor at the end of a helpline. Find someone you trust and let them know how bad things are. Don't let fear, shame, or embarrassment prevent you from seeking help. Just talking about how you got to this point in your life can release a lot of the pressure that's building up and help you find a way to cope.

Jaelline Jaffe, Ph.D., Lawrence Robinson, and Jeanne Segal, Ph.D. (updated April 2015) "Suicide Help: Dealing with Suicidal Thoughts and Feelings". www.helpguide.org. Used by permission.

Helps for Eating Disorders

Finding Balance Ministries
www.findingbalance.com

Freedom from Eating Disorders
Email: freedom6@freedomfromed.com
www.freedomfromed.com

Mercy Ministries Christian Residential Program (free of charge)
Phone: (615)831-6987
Email: info@mercyministries.com
US: www.mercyministries.com
Canada: www.mercyministries.ca

Vision of Hope Residential Treatment Center
Lafayette, Indiana
(765)447-5900
www.vohlafayette.org

Warning signs of an eating disorder
- Has an obsession with weight and food. It might seem like all your friend thinks (and talks) about is food, calories, fat grams, weight, and being thin.
- Feels the need to exercise all the time, even when sick or exhausted, and might talk about compensating for eating too much by exercising or burning off calories.
- Avoids hanging out with you and other friends during meals and always comes up with an excuse not to eat lunch at school or go out to eat.
- Starts to wear big or baggy clothes as a way to hide his or her body and shape.
- Goes on extreme or highly restrictive diets (for example, eating only clear soup or only raw veggies), cuts food into tiny pieces, moves food around on the plate instead of eating it, and is very precise about how food is arranged on the plate.
- Seems to compete with others about how little he or she eats. If a friend proudly tells you she only had a diet drink for breakfast and a few grapes for lunch, it's a red flag that she could be developing a problem.
- Goes to the bathroom a lot, especially right after meals, or you've heard your friend vomiting after eating.
- Always talks about how fat he or she is, despite losing a lot of weight, and sometimes focuses on body parts he or she doesn't like (such as the stomach, thighs, or arms) to the point of excess.
- Appears to be gaining a lot of weight even though you never see him or her eat much.
- Is very defensive or sensitive about his or her weight loss or eating habits.
- Buys or takes stimulants, diet pills, laxatives, steroids, herbal supplements, or other medicines to lose weight.
- Has a tendency to faint, bruises easily, is very pale, or starts complaining of being cold more than usual (this can be a symptom of being underweight).

Excerpted from: "I Think My Friend May Have an Eating Disorder: What Should I Do?" Reviewed by Michelle New, Ph.D. (Sept. 2014). www.kidshealth.org

Physical effects of anorexia nervosa
- Irreversible tooth decay and gum damage
- Damage to esophagus and larynx
- Slow heart rate, irregular heartbeat, heart failure
- Anemia (low red blood cell count which results in reduced oxygen to all areas of body)
- Impaired thinking ability, mood swings
- Hair thins and becomes brittle
- Bone loss (danger of fractures), weak muscles, swollen joints, osteoporosis
- Kidney stones, kidney failure
- Low potassium, magnesium, and sodium
- Irregular menstrual cycle or amenorrhea (no cycle), growth stunted, problems getting pregnant
- Skin bruises easily, gets cold quickly

Physical effects of bulimia nervosa
- Depression, dizziness, mood swings
- Cheeks swell, become sore
- Irreversible tooth decay and gum damage
- Throat and esophagus become sore/irritated; may eventually rupture or tear
- Irregular heartbeat, heart muscle weakened, heart failure
- Anemia
- Muscle fatigue
- Stomach pain, ulcers, may eventually rupture
- Dry skin
- Constipation, bloating, diarrhea, abdominal cramping, irregular bowel movements
- Dehydration, low potassium, magnesium, and sodium
- Irregular menstrual cycle or amenorrhea (no cycle)

What to do if you know someone who is struggling with an eating disorder:
- Find a non-threatening way to *ask about your friend's erratic behavior and apparent obsession with food.* Ask for clarification in case you observed incorrectly. Communicate your sincere desire to help your friend, as well as your serious concern for her safety and well being. Make sure she knows that you still care about her as a person and that you don't see her as a shameful problem needing a solution.

- *Be available to talk* whenever your friend needs to vent. Oftentimes, she can find a lot of emotional release and healing in verbalizing feelings, struggles, or fears. Listen carefully. While seeking to be compassionate and very sensitive toward your friend's pain, gently but firmly remind her that disordered eating can destroy her body, but won't solve her problems. Talk about God and the good purposes He has for his life, and the healing He wants to give her.

- *Encourage her to see a doctor and nutritionist for a full health evaluation.*

- *Encourage her to begin seeing a Christian counselor* regularly to receive practical steps toward proper, healthy thinking and decision-making.

- Above all, *pray continually for God to give you wisdom* to know what truths to share with your friend.

If you are struggling with an eating disorder:

- *Admit that you have a problem and need help overcoming it.* Until you can recognize and admit this, you will not benefit from the help others offer you.

-*Go to someone you trust and tell them what you are thinking and doing.*

-*See a medical doctor* for a full exam and tests to determine how your health may have been compromised, and what you need to take or do to regain good health. *Also consult a nutritionist* to create an eating plan for gradually restoring balanced, whole foods nutrition. You need to be open and specific with your doctor and nutritionist about your current eating habits, physical symptoms, and any stresses or abuse you are experiencing.

-*Make a plan of accountability with your friend*: Agree on steps to take when you feel tempted to starve, binge, purge, or compulsively overeat.

If you are looking at pornography:

Dirty Girls Ministries
Phone: (913)667-9492
www.dirtygirlsministries.com

Covenant Eyes Internet Accountability and Filtering
www.covenanteyes.com

If you need a counselor:

www.biblicalcounseling.com/counselors

If you want to get in touch with me:

Email: jhjost@gmail.com
www.purityandtruth.com
Facebook: Heidi Jost

Recommended Books

Depression
Hart, Archibald and Catherine Hart Weber. *Unveiling Depression in Women*
Lloyd-Jones, D. Martyn. *Spiritual Depression*
Welch, Edward T. *Depression: A Stubborn Darkness*

Disordered Eating and Body Image
Downs, Annie F. *Praising God from Head to Foot*
Rhodes, Constance. *Life Inside the 'Thin' Cage*
TerKeurst, Lysa. *Made to Crave*
Wierenga, Emily. *Chasing Silhouettes*

Pornography Addiction
Renaud, Crystal. *Dirty Girls Come Clean*
Hitz, Shelley and S'Ambrosia Curtis. *A Christian Woman's Guide to Breaking Free From Pornography*

Seeing the Real God
DeWitt, Steve. *Eyes Wide Open*
Freeman, Emily. *Grace for the Good Girl*
Keller, Timothy. *Counterfeit Gods* and *The Prodigal God*
Reeves, Michael. *Delighting in the Trinity*

Suicide
Hosier, Helen Kooiman. *An Eclipse of the Soul*

Endnotes

Dedication
3: *Alcott*: Louisa May Alcott, *Little Women*. New York: Grosset and Dunlap, 1963, 445.

Prologue
6: "There is no pit so deep": Corrie ten Boom, with John and Elizabeth Sherrill, *The Hiding Place*. New York: Bantam Books, 1971, 217.

Chapter 1: Beginnings
17: "[Katrina] told me about roller-skating": from a letter by Stephanie (Schuetz) Clark, written to me after Katrina died.

Chapter 2: Toned in Harmony
21: "The minds of the two girls": Charlotte Brontë, *Shirley*. Andrew and Judith Hook, eds., Penguin Books, 1974, 231.
28: "Do you know where": Timothy Keller, *King's Cross*. New York: Penguin, 2011, 147.

Chapter 3: Brick Walls, Fiery Angels, and Famine
42: "Women turn to food": Geneen Roth, *Women Food and God*. New York: Simon & Schuster, 2010, 32.
42: "We were made for more": Lysa TerKeurst, *Made to Crave*. Grand Rapids: Zondervan, 2010, 50.
43: "We're all walking around hungry": Geneen Roth, *When You Eat at the Refrigerator, Pull up a Chair. New* York: Hyperion, 1998, 48.
44: Habit loop: Charles Duhigg, *The Power of Habit*, chapter 3: The Golden Rule of Habit Change. New York: Random House, 2012. Kindle version.
44: "God's power is made perfect": TerKeurst, ibid. Pp. 103-104.
45: Lysa TerKeurst said: TerKeurst, ibid. p. 30.

Chapter 4: Glitter and Gold
48: "Everybody tells you": Katherine Sharpe, *Coming of Age on Zoloft*. Harper Perennial, 2012. Kindle version, Loc 3878.
48: "lose the protective covering": Archibald Hart and Catherine Hart Weber. A Woman's Guide to Overcoming Depression. Grand Rapids: Revell, 2002.
54: "A Wate-On ad": Lisa Wade, Ph. D., "Wate-On: True Beauty Includes a Full Figure." *The Society Pages*. Disqus, 25 Aug 2011. Web. 15 May 2015.
54: "An ad for Kelp-A-Mate": Wade, ibid.
"I am not going to teach": "Valeria Levitin, the World's Thinnest Woman Campaigns Against Anorexia." *The Citizens of Fashion*. 9 Jan 2013. Web. 15 May 2015.
54: "A study of Fijian girls": "Eating behaviors and attitudes following prolonged exposure to television among ethnic Fijian adolescent girls" (British Journal of Psychiatry, (2002) 180, 509-514)
55:"Do you really want to know why": Kylie Bisutti, *I'm No Angel*. Tyndale, 2013. Kindle version, Loc 1310.
55: "How can I be the big model?": Bisutti, ibid. Loc 1297.

55: "In an industry": Bisutti, ibid.
56: "Even when she cannot speak": Pamela Rosewell, *The Five Silent Years of Corrie ten Boom*. Grand Rapids: Zondervan, 1986, 177.

Chapter 5: Masked
64: "What, you too?": C.S. Lewis, *The Four Loves*. New York: Harcourt Brace, 1960, 97.
64: "culture of silence": Julia Lurie, "Speaking out on the problems within." *The Yale Herald*. Disqus, 5 November 2010. Web. 15 May 2015.
65: "Secure on the outside": Lisa Jost, *Fill Your Cup*. Jesus Free Us, 2012. Used by permission.
66: "We know that a habit": Duhigg, ibid. Loc 1498.
66: "For a habit to stay changed": Duhigg, ibid. Loc 1498.
67: "Come and rest in His mercy": Jost, ibid.

Chapter 6: Three Possible Paths
74: "What I do": Rom. 7:15.
75: "So if God is holy": Michael Reeves, *Delighting in the Trinity*. Downers Grove, IL: InterVarsity Press, 2012. Kindle version. Loc 1759.
75: "The Ruler and the problem is": Reeves, ibid. Loc 225.
76: "The nature of the triune God": Reeves, ibid. Loc 1026.
76: "We have inherent value": Bisutti, ibid. Loc 2981.
77: "We will always love": Reeves, ibid. Loc 1539.
78: "God created man": George Marsden, *Jonathan Edwards: A Life*. New Haven: Yale University Press, 2003, 98.

Chapter 7: Mountains and Giants
84: "I am by nature": Kevin Bywater.
84: "How can a young man": Ps. 119:9.
85: "If your brother is distressed": Rom. 14:15.
85: "Do not destroy": Rom. 14:20.
92: "we'll receive back a hundred times": Luke 18:29, 30.

Chapter 8: Collapsing Towers
99: "What is wrong for you": Shannon Ethridge and Stephen Arterburn, *Every Young Woman's Battle*. Colorado Springs: Waterbrook, 2004.
99: "Of the 40 million Americans": Shelley Hitz and S'ambrosia Curtis, *A Christian Woman's Guide to Breaking Free from Pornography*. Body and Soul Publishing, 2012. Kindle version. Loc 194.
99: "Seventeen percent of all women": Crystal Renaud, *Dirty Girls Come Clean*. Chicago: Moody Publishers, 2011. Kindle version. Loc 219.
99: "The thing about living": Renaud, ibid. Loc 296.
100: "An ever-increasing craving": C.S. Lewis, *The Screwtape Letters*. New York: Collier Books. 1982, 42.
100: "Surrender begins": Renaud, ibid. Loc 468.
101: "Confess your sins": Renaud, ibid. Loc 476.
101: "Accountability restores": Renaud, ibid. Loc 483.
101: "By accepting responsibility": Renaud, ibid. Loc 513.
101: "Sharing [your] story": Renaud, ibid. Loc 521.

Chapter 9: My Heart Grows Faint

120: "If you are trying": "Suicide Statistics." *Lost All Hope*. Web. 15 May 2015.

120: "A woman who shot herself": Helen Kooiman Hosier, *An Eclipse of the Soul.* Grand Rapids: Fleming H. Revell, 2005, 34.

120: "A man despairing": Did Bélizaire, of Quebec.

120: "A failed suicide attempt": Tai Marker, "My Long Road to Redemption After a Suicide Attempt." *Psych Central*. March 2013. Web. 15 May 2015.

122: "I picked up my phone": S, "Your Stories." *Lost All Hope*. July 2011. Web. 15 May 2015.

122: "*The Horse and His Boy*": C.S. Lewis, *The Chronicles of Narnia.* New York: HarperCollins, 2001, 281.

Chapter 10: Brown-Sugar Blessings

138: "Your time may come": J.R.R. Tolkien, *The Return of the King*. London: HarperCollins, 1999, 375-376.

142: "They shall grow not old": from Laurence Binyon's poem "For the Fallen" (1914), quoted in *Bonhoeffer: The Cost of Freedom,* Tyndale Entertainment, 1998.

145: "Later Life": Christina Rossetti, "Later Life" (1881). *About.Com: Classic Literature*. Web. 15 May 2015.

146: "Forlorn! The very word": John Keats, *Ode to a Nightingale*. In Paul McCormick, et al., eds. *Adventures in English Literature*. New York: Harcourt Brace, 1979, 534.

Chapter 11: It Is Sound

147: "Crowds gathered each week": Vernon C. Grounds, Our Daily Bread, Copyright 2005 by RBC Ministries, Grand Rapids, MI. Reprinted by permission. All rights reserved.

149: "But who shall so": Alfred, Lord Tennyson, "In Memoriam" (1850). *Bob's Byway*. Web. 15 May 2015.

Made in the USA
Middletown, DE
17 December 2015